VOLUME ONE

Comfort From

Meditations

For Such a Time as This

OLD TESTAMENT

NORTHWESTERN PUBLISHING HOUSE
Milwaukee, Wisconsin

Library of Congress Card 90-64-164
Northwestern Publishing House
1250 N. 113th St., Milwaukee, WI 53226-3284
© 1991 by Northwestern Publishing House
Published 1991
Printed in the United States of America

CONTENTS

Comfort for Troubled Lives

Faith Looks to the Future

Lessons from the School of Faith

Living in Security

Conversations with God

This Is Our Wonderful God

EDITOR'S PREFACE

For Such a Time as This. The title of this three volume set of devotions comes from a thought that Mordecai brought to Queen Esther's attention during days of trial and tribulation for the Old Testament people of God. "For such a time as this," Mordecai suggested, God had placed Esther in a position of honor and influence so she could bring God's promised help to God's people (Esther 4:14).

For Such a Time as This. Days of trial and tribulation are no strangers to God's people today. Trials and troubles challenge us, spiritual enemies beset us, fiery trials scorch our faith, our own frailty and mortality frightens us, tragic losses mount, guilt plagues our consciences, personal problems put us on the verge of despair, and sometimes even daily life seems difficult and discouraging.

For Such a Time as This. In times such as these Christians of all ages have turned to God in prayer seeking his help, his promised deliverance, his comfort. They have turned to his Word to find what he has to say to them, and for the past thirty-three years *Meditations* has helped to lead Christians to that comfort of God's Word. Comfort in the fact that God knows who we are, where we are, what we are. Comfort in that God knows the story of our lives and has seen to it through Jesus Christ that it has a happy ending. Comfort in that Jesus has promised to guide us through every trouble, even through the valley of the shadow of death, until we safely stand with him at God's right hand.

For Such a Time as This. Now 300 of those messages of comfort have been selected for inclusion in these three volumes. Each volume contains 100 devotions based on texts chosen from the Gospels, the Epistles, and the Old Testament. Pastor Henry Paustian of Watertown, Wisconsin read through some 12,045 devotions and selected the best of these comfort meditations. Minor changes have been made in some of the original devotions to bring them into line with current procedures. All Scripture quotations and citations are from the NIV; capitalization and punctuation principles reflect current style; titles now are solely the themes of individual devotions instead of a weekly series.

For Such a time as This. Note that on the cover the letters "h-i-s" in the word **this** are printed in another color. That was done to remind all of us that no matter in what situation we may find ourselves, this is still **his,** God's time, that our lives and the events in our lives happen not by chance but under the providential direction of our Father in heaven. As the cover illustration further indicates, we are always safe in his hands.

May the reader find God's comfort in these devotions.

Lyle Albrecht

Do you not know? Have you not heard? The LORD is the everlasting God, the Creator of the ends of the earth. He will not grow tired or weary, and his understanding no one can fathom. He gives strength to the weary and increases the power of the weak. Even youths grow tired and weary, and young men stumble and fall; but those who hope in the LORD will renew their strength. They will soar on wings like eagles; they will run and not grow weary, they will walk and not be faint. (Isaiah 40:28-31)

GOD PROVIDES STRENGTH FOR EACH DAY

"**G**od is not dead, nor doth he sleep," said the poet. God does not even get tired, the Prophet Isaiah adds in these words of our text. God is not dead, so we may enjoy living in our Father's world. God does not sleep, so we can lie down and rest in peace. He does not even get tired, so we can relax and let him run the universe!

He is strong and has strength to share. He will always provide today's strength for today's burdens and today's efforts. Do not try to take tomorrow's tensions and work, frustrations and anxiety, suffering and temptation today. Your God has not yet equipped you for tomorrow. You *can* cope today with today's load, for He is at your side, bearing you up. Tomorrow you will be able to cope with tomorrow's problems, because tomorrow He will give you the strength for that day.

Athletic coaches like to say: "When the going gets tough, the tough get going." Isaiah speaks of a time when even the tough might not be able to go any further, a time when "Even the youths shall faint and be weary, and the young men shall utterly fall." By his prophet the Lord assures us here that even when the youngest and toughest and strongest can neither keep going nor get going, then those who trust in him will receive new strength from him. The Apostle Paul wrote of the experiences he had undergone for the Gospel's sake. They were experiences that only a tough man could take and they would have stopped a man who lacked commitment. He wrote: "Though outwardly we are wasting away, yet inwardly we are being renewed day by day. When our outward life seems to be a struggle which we are losing, then God renews us inwardly. He comes in Word and Sacrament, in answer to prayer, as the gracious Father of his world. He helps and renews and bears us up on eagle's wings.

The athletic coach tells his young men to reach down into themselves for reserves of strength and energy. The prophet invites us here to reach up to the LORD for a supply of his strength. He has it to spare and to share.

Almighty Father, give us each day the strength for that day. Amen.

1

"When my life was ebbing away, I remembered you, LORD." (Jonah 2:7)

DO HEROES FAINT?

Heroes and heroines never quit! The more exhausted their bodies become, the more they seek within themselves for reserve strength. The body just won't give up because the spirit and mind push it to continue on. Observe the prize-fighter in the late rounds of the fight. Observe the farmer straining to clear the hay-field before the threatening storm arrives. This is the stuff of which heroes are made.

Jonah nearly quit. He just about gave up. The situation looked bleak. The waters of the sea surrounded him and closed in on him. Death seemed to encircle him, growing closer and closer with each breath. Any hope for escape dimmed with the passing moments. He was down in the dumps, giving up, fainting in his heart and soul. And what added to the feeling of weakness was the fact that he knew very well he had brought this whole situation upon himself.

But Jonah did not quit. He found new hope and strength. It was not in some inherent power which he suddenly remembered that he possessed. "I remembered the LORD," Jonah tells us. The faith in his Lord which filled his heart reminded him that he had a strength outside of himself, a strength he could look to and call on to sustain him and see him through his dilemma. Oh, how this remembering lifted up his heart and soul with new courage and strength! His faith prevented his fainting into despair.

Remember the Lord! What good and sound encouragement for us when we feel faint. "I can't do it," is the frustration every heart feels at times. It may be in times of danger. It may be at times of physical exhaustion or times of worry. It may be when our sins weigh heavily on us. Remember the Lord! He has paid for those sins. He has carried the burden for us. In our Lord Jesus we have the blessed invitation from God, "Cast your cares on the LORD, and he will sustain you" (Psalm 55:22).

Remember the Lord! His strength is made perfect in us when we are most weak in body or soul. Even if our outward man, our body, grows weak under the stresses of life or the burdens of old age, we faint not because "inwardly we are being renewed day by day" (2 Corinthians 4:16). It is nourished and strengthened by God's mighty Word. Remember the Lord, and faint not!

Lord, help me remember you to find strength when I feel faint. Amen.

(The Lord) hath sent me . . . to proclaim the year of the Lord's favor and the day of vengeance of our God, to comfort all who mourn, and provide for those who grieve in Zion—to bestow on them a crown of beauty instead of ashes, the oil of gladness instead of mourning, and a garment of praise instead of a spirit of despair. (Isaiah 61:2,3)

THE FORTIFIER

"I will praise the Lord no matter what happens" (Psalm 34:1-LB). Would you give such unconditional praise to God? Could you ever say that? Do you praise the Lord even though you have poor health, are in serious financial difficulties or have family problems? It is almost unbelievable that a sensible person would make such a statement.

And yet David did. And David was no stranger to troubles. He not only had the Philistines after him because he killed Goliath; he also had to contend with the envy and hatred of King Saul. King Saul tried to kill him on several occasions, pursued him mercilessly, so that David had no peace. David lost several children— one a baby, the others when grown.

David was also no stranger to temptation and sin. He fell into the sins of pride, adultery, lying and murder—to name just a few. Read 1 and 2 Samuel if you are interested in more details of the life of this saint-sinner King of Israel.

How could he under the circumstances of his life say, "I will praise the Lord no matter what happens"? How was David able to rise above sin and sorrow to victory and greatness?

The answer is in today's text. It points out that Jesus is the Fortifier. To fortify means to strengthen. If you find yourself weak and helpless, in need of strength and aid, then turn to Jesus. We do not find strength in ourselves, nor in the world, but in Jesus Christ. We mourn over our sin, our guilt and our mistakes. Jesus forgives our sin, removes our guilt, corrects our mistakes and gives us the ability to cope with life and death and eternity.

David was very realistic in his faith. He wrote in Psalm 34: 18,19: "The Lord is close to those whose hearts are breaking; he rescues those who are humbly sorry for their sins. The good man does not escape all troubles—he has them too. But the Lord helps him in each and every one" (LB). Believe and rejoice in Jesus your Fortifier!

Jesus, thank you for the faith and strength to cope with life. Amen.

If the LORD had not been on our side—let Israel say—if the LORD had not been on our side when men attacked us, when their anger flared against us, they would have swallowed us alive; the flood would have engulfed us, the torrent would have swept over us, the raging waters would have swept us away. Praise be to the LORD, who has not let us be torn by their teeth. We have escaped like a bird out of the fowler's snare; the snare has been broken, and we have escaped. Our help is in the name of the LORD, the Maker of heaven and earth. (Psalm 124)

OUR ONLY HOPE AND HELP

"I just don't know where to turn any more for help." Has this feeling ever crept into your heart? Have you ever felt that there was no help for you and your particular problem? Next time Satan puts this feeling into your heart, say confidently with the writer of Psalm 124, "Our help is in the name of the LORD."

The children of Israel had faced great difficulties and powerful enemies. The psalmist compares these to wild beasts ready to devour them, to a flood of waters about to engulf them and to a snare with the noose tightening around them. He confesses, "If it had not been the LORD who was on our side," we would have been overwhelmed. We were lost, hopelessly lost. But we found help with the Lord. Yes, "our help is in the name of the LORD, the Maker of heaven and earth."

The Lord is your only hope and help. When you feel that your spiritual enemies, the devil, the world and your flesh are about to devour you; when you feel that the floodwaters of doubt and uncertainty are about to drown you; when you feel that the very noose of unbelief is tightening around you, then remember: "our help is in the name of the LORD."

And if you wonder whether he is able to help, remember that he made heaven and earth. With him all things are possible. There is no problem so great that he can not solve it for you. There is no enemy so strong that he cannot defeat him. Even the greatest enemy of all, Satan, is not too strong for him. Christ has overcome the devil and the world, and he will help you overcome the temptations of your flesh.

So there is never cause for a Christian to doubt or to despair. Rather, when the minister reminds him in church every Sunday: "Our help is in the name of the LORD," he will express his confidence and trust by responding, "Who made heaven and earth."

Who trusts in God, a strong abode In heaven and earth possesses;
Who looks in love to Christ above, No fear his heart oppresses.
In Thee alone, dear Lord, we own Sweet hope and consolation,
Our Shield from foes, our Balm for woes, Our great and sure Salvation.
                                                                    Amen.

4

Therefore we will not fear, though the earth give way and the mountains fall into the heart of the sea, though its waters roar and foam and the mountains quake with their surging. (Psalm 46:2,3)

DON'T BE AFRAID!

To feel helpless is frightening. To fear for one's life is terrible. This psalm reminds us of such feelings in a striking way: the ground giving way beneath our feet, massive mountains quaking and toppling around us, plunging into the deepest part of the sea as the waters crash and roll together with earth-shattering force. The natural catastrophes of earth—earthquakes, tornadoes, floods, etc. remind us of how easily earthly security can give way to overwhelming disaster.

Even in an otherwise peaceful world, trouble may come—a severe accident, an illness, the loss of a family member or the loss of our job or home. On our own we are vulnerable and helpless in the face of evil. With dangers and trouble all around us, what hope can the Bible offer?

In this world we will have trouble. But in Christ we have a way through the evils of life, through its troubles and trials. God is our refuge and strength. Even when we walk through the valley of the shadow of death, we fear no evil, for our Good Shepherd is with us, leading the way. His word sets our hearts at ease as we entrust ourselves and all things into his almighty care. His grace restores our lives.

We can best cope with hard times by walking with Jesus every day. We draw courage and comfort from his Word. We call for his help in prayer. We learn to share our burdens with Christian friends, and in turn help and encourage others. Together as a church and on our own as individuals, we lay down every care at our Father's throne of grace.

How often God's angels told believers in the past, "Fear not! Don't be afraid!" God is our refuge. The Holy Spirit who first brought us to trust in Jesus preserves our faith through God's Word and sacraments. This heavenly assurance of peace with God sets us free from the shame and frustrations of sin. It moves us to trust fearlessly in God even in the midst of trouble. For we know that all things work together for the good of those who love God. We fix our eyes on Jesus, through whom we have become citizens of an eternal home which will never be lost or destroyed.

Even when the end of this world arrives, and the earth gives way to the fire of the judgment, we need not fear. For out of its destruction, we will arise with joy to live with our faithful Savior forever.

Thank you, Lord, for delivering me from every evil. Amen.

They cried to you and were saved; in you they trusted and were not disappointed. (Psalm 22:5)

WHERE IS YOUR GOD?

Disappointments, failures, tragedies make life hard, trying and bitter. Does God really care when we are in trouble? "Where is your God?" says the man of the world as misfortune and sorrow heap themselves on believers.

Trials and troubles seem to tumble in from all sides, making life difficult and discouraging. At times even the sinful heart of the Christian anxiously asks, "Where is God? Has he forgotten me?"

As the believer stands at the deathbed of a dear child and then at the grave, the thought surges through the mind: Does God really love me? As the Christian has one prop after another pulled out from under him, he asks: Has God turned from me?

See all the misery, loneliness, distress and destruction in the world! And sometimes it seems as though the Christian gets a double portion of it all. Does God care? Is he really my God?

"Where is your God?" There he hangs on Calvary's cross, dying because he cares. There Jesus shed his blood because he loves us and does not want us to perish. If God did not spare his own Son, but gave him into death to make us heirs of life eternal, then he certainly does care as we go through life. He will not leave us hopeless or helpless. Underneath are the everlasting arms of God, which will not let us fall.

When it comes right down to it, we really deserve nothing good at all from God. We deserve "nothing but punishment," as we confess every Sunday. Nevertheless, he abundantly pardons us through Christ. Jesus' blood blots out even the foulest deed. There is peace, hope and joy in Christ crucified. God will not accuse us or close the door on us, but will finally deliver our souls from death and hell.

So we can live joyfully through each day, knowing that our God will sustain us. We are not stumbling along on an aimless road, but in a direction that God wills to take us for our good. So we can sleep in safety each night under the shadow of his wings. The Lord is the Keeper of our body and the Lover of our souls. And he is the Ruler of the universe. We will never be disappointed for having put our trust in him.

Dearest Savior, teach me to appreciate your sacrifice on the cross. Remove all thoughts of rebellion and dissatisfaction from my heart and help me confess that your will is wiser than mine. In every problem, let your presence calm my spirit. Help me to know and to understand that you love me with an everlasting love. Amen.

But those who hope in the LORD **will renew their strength. They will soar on wings like eagles; they will run and not grow weary, they will walk and not be faint. (Isaiah 40:31)**

IN HIM WE SHALL OVERCOME

The problems that faced Israel in Isaiah's day were very much like those we face today. There was tension between nations with the ever-present possibility of war. The influence of pagan religion was disturbing Israel. Economic, social, political and religious differences are equally disruptive today. Include also the personal difficulties of making a living, trying to stay healthy and out of trouble, and putting forth all the emotional energy needed to stay on good terms with family, neighbors and fellow workers. Add up all the trying and difficult problems of life, and you have all the ingredients for being really tired—dead tired. It is no wonder that many people seek escape at some weekend retreat. Some divert their attention from worries through sports activities. Others may seek escape in drugs and alcohol.

Sad to say, most people tend to look in the wrong direction for relief from the sin-included tensions of life. That is why tensions are growing, not lessening. Isaiah has a solution for this sorry situation. He promises that those who wait upon the Lord, that is, those who believe in God's power to deliver us from any and all difficulty, shall be blessed with renewed strength. He uses an illustration from nature to picture God's help. As effortlessly as an eagle spreads its wings and lets currents of air lift it up to lofty heights, so the believer will be lifted up above all his problems, especially the problems of sin. He who trusts in God's salvation in Christ will "run" through life and not be weary. He will walk the walk of life with all its responsibilities and tensions and not grow faint.

Does all this sound too good to be true? Not to the Christian who has learned with St. Paul that he can do all things through Christ, who strengthens him. For that reason it is a distinct privilege and pleasure for us to go to church to worship our God and Savior, to sing of his blessings and to praise his holy name. And we eagerly listen to his Gospel, which assures us that in Christ God has cleansed us of our sin; in Christ we have overcome death and damnation.

Thy Word doth deeply move the heart,
Thy Word doth perfect health impart,
Thy Word my soul with joy doth bless,
Thy Word brings peace and happiness. Amen.

But now, this is what the LORD says—he who created you, O Jacob, he who formed you, O Israel: "Fear not, for I have redeemed you; I have summoned you by name; you are mine. When you pass through the waters, I will be with you; and when you pass through the rivers, they will not sweep over you. When you walk through the fire, you will not be burned; the flames will not set you ablaze. (Isaiah 43:1,2)

THE PROTECTED LIFE

Famous persons and public officials are not the only people exposed to danger. Every one of us faces the possibility of injury, sickness and death. When we Christians experience such things in our lives, we may be troubled as to whether the Lord really is protecting us. Luther says in the explanation to the First Article that God is "defending me against all danger, and guarding and protecting me from all evil." If the Lord is at our side, how can evil happen to us?

This is not a new question. It was often asked by the people of Israel. Many of the psalms raise questions about the Lord's care and concern for his people. What was God's answer to Israel? What is his answer to us?

Public figures often have their body guards. Candidates for the presidency are protected by the secret service. Yet we know from experience that there is no foolproof protection. If someone is really determined to hurt or harm another person, he will at times be successful despite all protective efforts.

The words of Isaiah in our text are addressed to the people of Israel who are suffering in the Babylonian captivity. This is a word from the Lord to a nation created, redeemed and called by him. This is a word from the Lord to people who belong totally to him.

What is his promise? He does not say they will not go through any "waters" or walk through any "fire." Water and fire are symbols of the dangers and evil surrounding people. Fire is often used as a symbol for punishment and destruction. The Lord does allow trouble to come to us. We are exposed to dangers, to injury, to sickness, to death.

Yet the Lord protects us by bringing us through these dangers and troubles. He brings us through the deep waters of earthly trials and tribulations. The Lord says to his own dear children, "I will be with you. You will not drown in the deep waters. You will not be scorched by the fire." With the Lord walking at our side, we will reach the goal of our journey unharmed.

Gracious Savior, comfort me with the assurance that you will be with me in all danger, trouble and sickness. Amen.

8

Yours, O LORD, is the greatness and the power and the glory and the majesty and the splendor, for everything in heaven and earth is yours. (1 Chronicles 29:11)

THE COMFORT OF GOD'S POWER

A "weather rock" hangs by a rope from a tripod along a road on Washington Island in Lake Michigan. A sign is tacked up next to the "weather rock." It tells how to use the rock to tell the weather. If the rock is wet, it is raining. If the rock feels cold, it is cold. If the rock is white, it is snowing. The sign continues on and on and at the end it reads, "The wonderful thing about this 'weather rock' is that it is not affected by the weather." The implication is that we human beings are unlike the rock. We are affected by the weather and by our environment and by all of God's creation.

Because we in this world are affected by cold and heat, prosperity and disaster, these words of 1 Chronicles are so comforting: "Everything in heaven and earth is yours." God is the creator of all things. Everything that is exists with his knowledge and by his creation. Because God loves us, all things created are for our good.

But sin has corrupted all things. Sin has ruined the goodness of God's creation. But sin has not destroyed God's love for all people. "For God so loved the world that he gave his one and only Son, that whoever believes in him shall not perish but have eternal life" (John 3:16).

God loves us. He cares for us. He knows that we are not "weather rocks" unaffected by the storms and troubles of this life. Therefore God gives us his promises found in his Word: "In all things God works for the good of those who love him" (Romans 8:28). "He who did not spare his own Son, but gave him up for us all—how will he not also, along with him graciously give us all things?" (Romans 8:32)

These are the promises of the almighty God who created all things and who governs all things. He loves us. We praise our almighty God for the comfort of his power which he uses out of love for our eternal good. "Yours, O LORD, is the greatness and the power and the glory and the majesty and the splendor, for everything in heaven and earth is yours."

O Lord, since all things are yours, protect us in this sinful world in your love and mercy by your great power. Amen.

Abraham fell facedown; he laughed and said to himself, "Will a son be born to a man a hundred years old? Will Sarah bear a child at the age of ninety?" (Genesis 17:17) Sarah . . . bore a son . . . at the very time God had promised him. . . . Sarah said, "God has brought me laughter, and everyone who hears about this will laugh with me." (Genesis 21:2,6)

REASSURANCE FOR DOUBTING HEARTS

This laughter of Sarah and Abraham is the same joy and happiness that lives in our hearts when we know that God's promises are sure and that his promises apply to us. We rejoice when we finally come to see that even during our times of trouble and doubt God was with us to take care of things and make them work out for our good.

This joy and laughter are a response that comes from a faith that has just been uplifted by God's repeated promises and their fulfillment. In Abraham's case his faith came to rejoice in God's promises even before their fulfillment. Sarah's joy was complete when she saw that God truly did bring to pass everything he had promised.

We can also laugh with Sarah when we recognize that this whole story can serve to reassure our doubting hearts. It can move us to reason, "If God was faithful to his promise to Abraham and Sarah, will he not also be faithful to the promises he has made to us in his Word?"

Here God performed a mighty miracle to keep the promise of the Savior. He had promised the Savior of the world was to come from the family of Abraham and Isaac. If Isaac had not been born, that family line would have ended and along with it the promise of a Savior. If it took a miracle to bring this important child to these two old people, then God would provide the miracle.

If 2,000 years later it would take a miracle for Jesus to be born of a virgin, then God would provide another miracle. If it would even be necessary for God to leave heaven to come to earth to save mankind, then this is what God would do. He did, and Jesus who is God came to earth for our salvation.

Jesus is the reason we can laugh and sing for joy. Jesus is the reason the fear of death and hell has been replaced with joy and hope. God let nothing stop him from bringing the Savior into the world. Let us rejoice in our Savior. He wishes the laughter of faith to be found in our home.

I will greatly rejoice in the Lord, my soul shall be joyful in my God, for he hath clothed me with garments of salvation, he hath covered with the robe of righteousness. Amen.

For men are not cast off by the LORD forever. Though he brings grief, he will show compassion, so great is his unfailing love. (Lamentations 3:31,32)

GOD'S TIME IS THE BEST TIME

"**H**ow long will this suffering continue?" This is a question which many a Christian has asked during periods of severe testing. And yet his very suffering can serve as a source of real comfort to him. Scripture makes this point repeatedly. The Bible is lined with comforting passages which become especially precious to those who are experiencing the chastening rod of God. Job, for example, who endured afflictions far greater than any we will ever have to bear, was comforted by the knowledge that, "When he has tested me, I will come forth as gold" (Job 23:10). The Apostle Paul, who experienced numerous tribulations himself, encourages us to "rejoice in our sufferings," because "suffering produces perseverance; perseverance, character; and character, hope" (Romans 5:3,4).

So leave everything up to the Lord! His time is the best time when it comes to bestowing blessings of joy as well as blessings of affliction.

The psalmist writes, "Out of the depths I cry to you, O LORD; O LORD, hear my voice. Let your ears be attentive to my cry for mercy. If you, O LORD, kept a record of sins, O LORD, who could stand? But with you there is forgiveness; therefore you are feared. I wait for the LORD, my soul waits, and in his word I put my hope. My soul waits for the LORD more than watchmen wait for the morning, more than watchmen wait for the morning. O Israel, put your hope in the LORD, for with the LORD is unfailing love and with him is full redemption. He himself will redeem Israel from all their sins" (Psalm 130).

When we remember that the Lord "will have compassion according to the multitude of his mercies," our thoughts include, but also soar above, the many temporal blessings which we sinners receive from him in this world of sin. We fix our gaze upon the compassionate Christ, who bestows eternal blessings on those who are oppressed by sin and guilt —for he has removed our sin and guilt and the cause of all suffering. In him we have conquered sin and death and Satan and hell.

When we are reminded by the theme for today that "God's time is the best time," how can we forget that best "time" of all, the "fullness of the time" when God sent forth his Son to redeem the world! The redemptive work of this Son of God makes it easy for us to endure the tribulations of life on earth, for we look ahead in confident faith to the endless bliss of heaven!

To you, O God and Savior, we give all praise and honor. Amen.

Who has understood the mind of the LORD, or instructed him as his counselor? Whom did the LORD consult to enlighten him, and who taught him the right way? Who was it that taught him knowledge or showed him the path of understanding? (Isaiah 40:13,14)

QUESTIONING GOD'S WAYS

"**L**ord, sometimes I just don't understand you. Just when our income is already strained, the washing machine breaks down. When I could be teaching Sunday school, this illness keeps me in bed. You have promised what is best for me, but, Lord, this is hard to understand." Does this sound like us at times? Often because we do not understand God's ways, we are tempted to doubt the wisdom of God's dealings with us. There are many things we don't understand about God.

Job, an Old Testament believer, found himself questioning God's way of doing things. Job was suffering a prolonged hardship when his questioning of God's wisdom began. Emphatically God asked Job, "Where were you when I laid the earth's foundation? Tell me, if you understand" (Job 38:4). Job was unable to respond. God thus taught him the truth of the words, "For my thoughts are not your thoughts, neither are your ways my ways," declares the LORD (Isaiah 55:8).

The text of today's meditation is a similar reminder from God when we begin to question the wisdom of his dealings with us. We are asked, "Who has directed the Spirit of the Lord? Who was his counselor? Who taught him justice, knowledge, understanding?" The answer: No one. The lesson: God's wisdom, knowledge, understanding and his way of doing things are supreme. The heroes and heroines of faith didn't always understand God's will for their lives. But they trusted his wisdom, his knowledge, his judgment and his foresight. With a childlike faith they learned that "God moves in a mysterious way, his wonders to perform."

There will be times when we just don't understand God's will for our lives or his ways of dealing with a loved one. It is at such moments that we will be comforted by remembering how his wisdom far excels ours. In time, like Joseph, we will discover that even the most perplexing and disastrous events can become a source of blessings from God—from a loving God, who knew in advance the result.

Dear Lord, forgive us for doubting your wisdom and your manner of dealing with us. May the knowledge that you know all things be a comfort to us. Teach us to pray, "Lord, I don't understand, but I do believe." We thank you for the blessings you have bestowed upon us, especially faith in Jesus Christ as our Savior. Amen.

I will not die but live, and will proclaim what the LORD has done. The LORD has chastened me severely, but he has not given me over to death. (Psalm 118:17,18)

IF A MAN DIES, WILL HE LIVE AGAIN?

In the midst of life we are in death. As we see people, the young and the old, one by one leave the land of the living, there arises the question, "If a man dies, shall he live again?"

Yes, says Jesus. But even more. The resurrection day of Jesus Christ makes me sure that I shall not die, but live.

I shall not die eternally. Eternal death, the fearful wages of sin, with all its hellish torments, has lost its power over believers. Christ has abolished it. He has brought life and immortality to light. Jesus said of himself: "I am the Resurrection and the Life." He proved that claim. Not only did he raise Lazarus from the dead and restore life to him, he also laid down his life for our sins and took it up again to confirm his words as true.

This is the same Jesus who says to us: "Because I live, you shall live also." "He who believes in me will live, even though he dies; and whoever lives and believes in me will never die."

Of course, the prospect of physical death faces all of us. Our body will then corrupt in the grave. But we shall rise from the dead. Christ will fashion our vile body like unto his glorious body, and we shall see him as he is, for we shall be like him and live with him eternally in his home of glory.

This is our resurrection hope, glorious, comforting and sure. As death and the grave could not hold Jesus, so it cannot hold those who die trusting in him. Christ is the first fruits of them that slept. The full resurrection harvest of all believers will follow when Christ comes again at the last day.

This hope which we have in Christ, however, has meaning for us during this life as well. With this sure hope of life in Christ, we do not despair under adversity and affliction. God may indeed let trials, afflictions, pain and suffering come upon us. We know, however, why he does this. In his love he is only chastening us, for whom the Lord loves, he chastens. He wants to correct us when we sin, so that we are not condemned with the world. He wants to exercise our faith in humble trust and patience, and draw our eyes upward to that untroubled life he has prepared for us in heaven.

Therefore, even as he chastens us, we are confident that he has not given us over to death, that we should suffer eternally. With unshaken faith in our risen Savior, we will go on to declare the works of the Lord and praise him for the marvels of his mercy both here in time and hereafter in eternity.

Abide with us; with heav'nly gladness
Illumine, Lord, our darkest day;
And when we weep in pain and sadness,
Be Thou our Solace, Strength, and Stay.
Tell of Thy woe, Thy vict'ry won,
When Thou didst pray: "Thy will be done." Amen.

So the two women went on until they came to Bethlehem. When they arrived in Bethlehem, the whole town was stirred because of them, and the women exclaimed, "Can this be Naomi?" "Don't call me Naomi," she told them. "Call me Mara, because the Almighty has made my life very bitter. I went away full, but the LORD has brought me back empty. Why call me Naomi? The LORD has afflicted me; the Almighty has brought misfortune upon me." (Ruth 1:19-21)

LOOKING TO A HAPPY ENDING

Why do some of God's children seem to have such unhappy and miserable lives? A good person to ask would be Naomi, mother-in-law of Ruth. Remember her story.

There was a severe famine in Israel. Naomi, her husband Elimelech, and their two sons were forced to leave their home in Bethlehem and immigrate to the country of Moab across the Jordan River. But this new land did not give the family the happiness it sought. Elimelech died very soon. The rest of the family still stayed in Moab. His two sons married Moabite women, Ruth and Orpah. Then unexpectedly the two sons also died.

Ten years after leaving Bethlehem, Noami returned. She left with an empty stomach; she returned with an empty heart. She left with a husband and two sons; she returned with a daughter-in-law. And she was a Moabite. Her old friends hardly recognized sad Naomi. No wonder she told them, "Don't call me Naomi (Gracious). Call me Mara (Bitter)."

We can readily understand Naomi's bitterness. All she could see at her homecoming was her past suffering and sorrow. She had lost her husband and sons. Their life in Moab was a failure. She was destitute. It seemed like even God was against her.

But we know how the story turned out. We can read ahead and find out that Ruth becomes a greater blessing to her mother-in-law than a dozen sons. We know that in time Naomi would hold in her arms a grandson. He was destined to be the grandfather of great King David and the ancestor of David's greater Son, the Savior Jesus Christ. However Naomi could see none of this at her return.

As with Naomi, God in his all-knowing wisdom does not allow us to look into our future either. So then it is not surprising that sometimes we too are inclined to bitterness. When we look backward at deaths in the family, loss of a job, failure in school or rejection by a loved one, it becomes rather easy to blame God.

We can only look at the past, God knows the future. Our heavenly Father already knows the story of our life. And he has seen to it that through Jesus Christ it has a happy ending—in heaven.

Gracious God, remove all bitterness and fill me with your love. Amen.

I know that my Redeemer lives, and that in the end he will stand upon the earth. And after my skin has been destroyed, yet in my flesh I will see God; I myself will see him with my own eyes—I, and not another. How my heart yearns within me! (Job 19: 25-27)

FAITH THAT LOOKS TO THE FUTURE

Job was sure he was dying. He was in agony. His strength had completely left him. All hope of recovery was gone. What was left? Job's only comfort was the living hope of the resurrection.

There is nothing that helps a Christian through difficult days more than meditating on the resurrection. Christ is risen, and so we too shall rise. It's a glorious future that awaits us in heaven. That sunbeam of eternity can pierce through any gloom and misery which weigh us down now.

The thing that's so remarkable about Job was that he could express so clearly the same hope we have. Even though he lived hundreds of years before Christ rose from the dead, he could see with eyes of faith his living Redeemer standing on the earth at the last day.

With those same spiritual eyes he could see himself in front of the Savior, looking at him with his own eyes, his bones once more clothed with flesh, ready to hear the blessed invitation of Christ: "Come, you who are blessed by my Father; take your inheritance, the kingdom prepared for you since the creation of the world" (Matthew 25:34).

That faith which Job had is the same faith we need when everything seems to fall apart. When death itself appears to be at the door, it is our hope of the life to come with Christ that sustains us. A faith which looks to the future can say with Paul, "I consider that our present sufferings are not worth comparing with the glory that will be revealed in us" (Romans 8:18).

Can we see that glory? Can we look beyond the grave with Job to the day when our bodies will be raised and made like Christ's own glorious body? Can we fix our vision on the day when we will see the Lord with those same eyes that so often see only misery and suffering on this earth? Job conquered all with his triumphant faith in the resurrection. We can too.

Dear Lord, let me see your Son on the glorious day of the resurrection and hear his invitation to the blessings of heaven. Amen.

The LORD blessed the latter part of Job's life more than the first. (Job 42:1,2)

STORM CLOUDS ON THE ROAD TO HEAVEN

The air is never so fresh and full of zest as after the storm. The air is cool, the atmosphere clear and the sun is radiant. That's true after the spiritual storms that strike us also pass. After coming to the brink of despair on account of illness, financial reverses or spiritual depression, the Lord blesses us more at the end than at the beginning as he did Job.

After hiding his face behind the black clouds of suffering, once more God lets the sunshine of his love flood over us and we are overwhelmed with the consciousness of the goodness of the Lord. The person who was oppressed with an overpowering sense of guilt and sinfulness suddenly realizes that it's really true that where sin abounded, grace abounds much more.

Job's suffering had an end. Job once had been the greatest man in the east. Now we read that the Lord blessed him with twice as much as he had in the first place. Job saw that the Lord had not cast him away forever but rather had purified him like fine gold, so that the glory of his faith shone brighter at the end than at the beginning.

Our trials and sufferings will also have an end. All Christians may say with confidence, "Even though I walk through the valley of the shadow of death, I will fear no evil, for you are with me; your rod and your staff, they comfort me." The road on which the Lord leads us is still the road to heaven. Job, Noah, Abraham, Jacob, Joseph, Moses and David all passed through dark days of trial, but all basked again in the Lord's favor. We can look back on past difficulties in our lives and must confess that the Lord has delivered us from them all.

Finally, after the trials of this life have passed and our faith like Job's shall have triumphed by the power of the Holy Spirit, we have the sure promise of God's Word: "He will wipe every tear from their eyes. There will be no more death or mourning or crying or pain, for the old order of things has passed away" (Revelation 21:4).

Surely, our end will also be greater than anything we have ever experienced up until now. "You have heard of Job's perseverance and have seen what the Lord finally brought about. The Lord is full of compassion and mercy" (James 5:11). Follow Job, then, in patient suffering to the abundant blessing which inevitably follows.

Lord, deliver us from all evil and finally for Jesus' sake receive us into the eternal happiness of heaven. Amen.

Rejoice greatly, O Daughter of Zion! Shout, Daughter of Jerusalem! See, your king comes to you. (Zechariah 9:9)

JOY IN THE MIDST OF PROBLEMS

At the time Zechariah wrote these words, there was little to rejoice about. The people of Judah had recently returned from captivity in Babylon. Work on the Temple had been halted by Samaritan opposition. The Jews had fallen into disfavor with the ruling Persian monarchs. God's people had become spiritually lethargic. To rouse his people to action and also to comfort them, the Lord sent the prophets Zechariah and Haggai. In the midst of Judah's gloom, Zechariah cried out, "Rejoice! Your king comes to you." God would send his Son to rescue them. This was cause for rejoicing.

The people of Jesus' day also lived in depressing times. They were under the domination of the Roman government. Tax collectors overcharged them and made their lives miserable. The religious leaders of the day misled and oppressed the people. Yet, in the midst of this gloom Christ brought joy. When he was born on Christmas, the angels filled the fields of Bethlehem with their songs of joy. God's Son had become flesh. This was a cause for rejoicing. When the aged Simeon beheld the Christchild, he joyfully praised the Lord.

Wherever Jesus went, he brought joy into the lives of sinners. Whether they were publicans, like Zacchaeus or Matthew, or the woman taken in adultery or the blind Bartimaeus, Jesus brought joy into their lives. The joy he brought was not a mere surface emotion that soon left them. Rather, Jesus brought joy based on the forgiveness of sins and the certainty of eternal life.

In our day, people also live in depressing circumstances. People have financial problems, health problems, marital problems and a host of other problems. People may be victimized by crime, unemployed, or socially disadvantaged. We all point to a number of things that are perplexing to us. But whatever problems we may have, we still have every reason to be happy and filled with joy. Jesus came to save us from death and hell. We are the children of God through faith in him. Our King made it possible for us to reign with him in heaven. We shall live forever in the presence of our King before his throne. There is no greater joy than this.

"Hosanna in the highest!" That ancient song we sing,
For Christ is our Redeemer, the Lord of heaven our King.
Oh, may we ever praise Him with heart and life and voice
And in His blissful presence eternally rejoice! Amen.

The LORD their God will save them on that day as the flock of his people. (Zechariah 9:16)

THE GOOD SHEPHERD LEADS US HOME

Sheep are very helpless animals. They are not intelligent. They cannot outwit their enemies. They do not have sharp hoofs to ward off an enemy's attack. They do not have sharp teeth to tear at the flesh of an attacking animal. They do not have great speed to outrun predators. They really have only one means of defense, and that is the shepherd. If it were not for the faithful shepherd, the sheep would soon perish.

It is no coincidence that Scripture frequently compares us with sheep. We, too, are helpless. In and of ourselves we cannot stand against the attacks of the devil, the world and our own sinful flesh. If it were not for the constant care of our Lord we also would perish.

It is with good reason that Jesus is called "the Good Shepherd." The prophet Ezekiel foretold the fact that the shepherd of God's people would be a king descended from the line of David (Ezekiel 34:23,24). Zechariah prophesied that this shepherd would be struck down (13:7), sold for 30 pieces of silver (11:12) and pierced through (12:10). All of this coincides with the words of Jesus, "I am the Good Shepherd. The Good Shepherd lays down his life for the sheep" (John 10:11). Jesus not only cares for his flock's physical needs, he has taken care of their greatest need— the need for forgiveness. He did this by his death on the cross and resurrection from the dead.

Though his lifeless body was in the grave for a brief time, Jesus rose from the dead triumphant on the third day. We, the members of his flock, have assurance that he lives to preserve us as his own until we stand with him in heaven. There the glorious vision of St. John will be fulfilled, "For the Lamb at the center of the throne will be their shepherd; he will lead them to springs of living water. And God will wipe away every tear from their eyes" (Revelation 7:17).

When we become frightened by the troubles in our lives and our own frailty, let us turn our eyes to our King, our Good Shepherd. He says to us, "My sheep listen to my voice; I know them, and they follow me. I give them eternal life, and they shall never perish; no one can snatch them out of my hand" (John 10:29).

> The Lord my Shepherd is,
> I shall be well supplied.
> Since He is mine and I am His,
> What can I want beside? Amen.

On that day the LORD will shield those who live in Jerusalem, so that the feeblest among them will be like David. (Zechariah 12:8)

STRENGTH FOR GOD'S PEOPLE

There are times, places and conditions that cause us to feel helpless, hopeless and powerless. In such circumstances the very thought of having enough strength to meet and overcome those things which make us feel feeble is beautiful. To be the possessor of an infallible promise which guarantees a time of strength fills us with joy, hope and peace. How one yearns to be so blessed at such times.

The people of God at Zechariah's time were in a most difficult and discouraging situation. There seemed to be no light in the darkness which was settling on them. They seemed to have no future. Everything seemed hopeless. They needed some inspiration. They needed some hope.

In our text God sets before his people that which they needed so desperately. He urges them not to look so much at themselves and their troubles but to lift up their eyes and look to the wonderful blessings in the day of the Messiah. That day would come. Its fulfillment would be total bliss and perfection in heaven.

There the salvation of God would completely fill God's people and strengthen them. Then all weakness would be gone. The most feeble would be royalty like David, the great king. Each of God's people would then be crowned with everlasting glory, honor and power. No matter how discouraging or hopeless things might seem, God's people were to take heart. God's promise of the day of the Messiah was true. He would come and give to his people the glory of heaven.

Such a message is vital for us of today also. There are so many things that trouble us, so many that confront us, so many dangers which threaten and worry us. Sometimes we all feel that we cannot go on and that we have no hope, no future. We become worried, afraid and feeble. At such times we need to listen to God speak through Zechariah of the coming eternal day of royal majesty and glory.

Through Christ this day is yours and mine now. We need to lift up our eyes to see our glorious future and by faith to walk onward in joy, strength, hope and peace. God in love pledged that day would come. God's Son lived, died and rose that it would be ours by faith in him. Therefore, people of God, listen to your God and be strengthened. Lift up your eyes and be encouraged. Walk onward in faith as those who are royalty and who will be like David in heaven.

Lord, let the spirit of David be ours in life, his glory be ours in death. Amen.

"And you will go out and leap like calves released from the stall. Then you will trample down the wicked; they will be ashes under the soles of your feet on the day when I do these things," says the LORD Almighty." (Malachi 4:2,3)

AWAITING THE DAY OF VICTORY

If you've ever lived on a farm or visited one at the right time, you probably have seen one of the most amusing things that can happen there. In the winter, the young cattle are put in barns to protect them from the bitter cold outside. They stay there until spring comes when they are let loose into the pasture. The moment the doors and gates are opened, those young calves take off for the wide open spaces like a bunch of clowns. They kick their heels high in the air and dance in circles. They act as if they were the happiest creatures God ever made.

In our passage for today, Malachi compares the joy of those who believe in Christ as their personal Savior from sin, death and hell, to the joy of those released calves. Even while living here on earth, we have already experienced that joy. It's the deep happiness that comes from knowing that our souls are secure for eternity—safe in the hands of Jesus our Lord. But that joy has only just begun.

Everything is not perfect yet. Being a believer and follower of Jesus is not *all* sunshine and roses.

We find that we are continually plagued by enemies—there is that unbelieving person who regularly pokes fun at our faithfulness to the Lord. There is the old evil Foe himself, Satan, who is always trying to tempt us to sin, and succeeding far too often. And there is one final enemy—death. These enemies are terrifying—and powerful. Who are we to cope with them?

But God promises us in this passage that these enemies shall one day be totally put down. They will be as powerless on the great day of the Lord as the dirt we walk on.

The Lord has already won the victory. When Jesus rose from the dead on Easter morning, he gave us visible proof that he had the power to conquer all our enemies—even death.

We have a share in that victory through faith in Christ as our Savior. For us it's only a matter of time until we sit at the victory table with our Lord in heaven. When judgment day comes, we will experience firsthand what it means to have absolutely perfect happiness and joy forevermore. That day may be very soon.

Alleluia! Alleluia! Alleluia! The strife is o'er, the battle done; now be the song of praise begun. Alleluia!

"The Redeemer will come to Zion, to those in Jacob who repent of their sins," declares the LORD. (Isaiah 59:20)

THE MEANING OF CHRIST'S VICTORY FOR US

What comfort to know we will surely obtain the glory which Jesus won for us. Clinging to that Victor we can exult in a world of strife. If God is for us—and Calvary's cross shows he is—who can be against us?

But can our conscience exult, recalling our rebellion against him? The blood of Jesus Christ, God's Son, cleanses us from all sin. Our sins are completely removed.

Can the legions of hell overcome us? The Redeemer came and he destroyed Satan's power forever. That's final!

Can our evil nature triumph over us? The unbreakable Word shows us that, "if anybody does sin, we have one who speaks to the Father in our defense—Jesus Christ, the Righteous One" (1 John 2:1). He has washed all our scarlet guilt white as snow, and made it spotless as fleecy wool.

Can affliction gain supremacy over us? Paul challenges, "Who shall separate us from the love of Christ? Shall trouble or hardship or persecution or famine or nakedness or danger or sword?" (Romans 8:35)

Because what seem losses to us come as proof of God's love, we can battle disaster and cry out, "No, in all these things we are more than conquerors through him who loved us" (Romans 8:37).

More than conquerors of sin.

More than conquerors of evil thoughts.

More than conquerors of the hostile world.

More than conquerors of temptations.

More than conquerors of doubt.

More than conquerors of death.

We can challenge, "Where, O death, is your victory? Where, O death, is your sting?" (1 Corinthians 15:55)

We have won with Christ. He is the Savior of all. He stands at our side. He meets every need. He has defeated every enemy of our soul once and for all.

Let us build our hope on him. As truly as he is the Son of God, victory is ours. We will face enemies, of course. Yet, with Jesus we will not fight alone. He will help us overcome and obtain the victory.

Jesus, stand at my side every minute of every day to assure me of redemption through your precious blood. Then whatever comes on life's battlefield, I will win with you. Amen.

For the LORD watches over the way of the righteous, but the way of the wicked will perish. (Psalm 1:6)

TRUE JOY HERE—TRUE JOY HEREAFTER

Fellow Christian, be happy! God knows you! He knows the way of the righteous. God laid out the way for us. He called us to it by his Gospel. His Spirit enlightened us to faith with his gifts. He keeps us in that way. "We are God's workmanship, created in Christ Jesus to do good works, which God prepared in advance for us to do" (Ephesians 2:10). How clearly Jesus points to that evidence of God's work in the lives of the righteous. He shows how they walked the way of faith and performed the good works ordained for them.

Be happy even if at times you feel that God doesn't know. You have the privilege to talk things over with him in prayer. Tell him your troubles or your needs at these times. Mary and Martha did that when their brother was ill. They informed Jesus, "Lord, the one you love is sick." They felt: If Jesus knows, he will do what is best and right. They were happy to let it go at that. Remember, even when the way of the righteous is rocky and thorny, be happy. God knows the way he leads. He has numbered the very hairs of your head, and you will not lose a single one without his knowledge.

Be happy. God assures you that everything upon your way will work together for your good. He leads you so that in the end he may invite you to come to his right hand and inherit the kingdom prepared for you from the foundation of the world. He will make you a king! He will greet you and say, "Here is your palace; it is prepared just for you."

Senior citizen, you say you feel forsaken at times? Be happy! You are never alone. He is with you and knows you so well that he calls you by your name. When the time is right, he will ask you to come to him.

Teen-ager, you are suffering ridicule for Christ? Be happy! You are not standing alone; Jesus knows your stand and confession. He is with you and will see you through to victory. He will confess you before his Father.

You who are away from home, in service, in school. Do you feel that the world is against you? Are temptations powerful? God has not forsaken you. He knows. Cling to him in faith, and you will be happy to all eternity.

To Christians everywhere God says, "I know you, you are mine own. Though sin and Satan seek to fell you, rejoice! Your home is with the blest."

Jesus, in mercy bring us
To that dear land of rest.
Who art, with God the Father
And Spirit, ever blest. Amen.

Therefore my heart is glad and my tongue rejoices; my body also will rest secure, because you will not abandon me to the grave. (Psalm 16:9,10)

SAFE EVEN IN DEATH

There is no greater reason for fear and insecurity than the fear of death. Today that fear has been increased by the threat of nuclear war. Every time we hear of the death of a relative or friend, we are reminded of the certainty of our own death. Even if we are young, we never know whether or not today is our last day on earth. It is certainly inevitable and even proper that we have fear of death. Death is not natural. It is a result of the curse of sin. Death is the tearing apart of body and soul, which God created to be together. Death is an enemy to be defeated and overcome. Indeed, death is the last and most terrible enemy which we must confront.

But thanks be to God, we cannot be defeated even by this terrible enemy. Because Christ has defeated Satan, sin and death, death cannot destroy us. Death cannot separate us from God and his love. Even in death our body and soul will be kept safe until they are united again on the day of resurrection. Both body and soul will be kept safe, but in different ways.

When we die, our soul returns to God, its creator. The souls of unbelievers go to hell to await judgment, but the souls of the believers are taken to heaven to be kept safe in the presence of God. Scripture does not give us much information about what the souls in heaven feel or experience between death and the day of resurrection, but we know that they are safe and enjoying a peaceful rest with God.

Although our body decays and returns to the ground from which it was created, we can speak of the death of the body as a sleep. The point of the comparison is that when we lie down to sleep at night we expect to wake up in the morning. When we place a lifeless body in the grave, we do so with the confidence that Jesus will wake that body to life on the day of resurrection. With his almighty power he will be able to restore that body no matter how it has dissolved or has been scattered in the meantime. Since we have this knowledge, not even the fear of death can overwhelm us.

Lord, let at last Thine angels come,
To Abram's bosom bear me home,
That I may die unfearing;
And in its narrow chamber keep
My body safe in peaceful sleep
Until Thy reappearing. Amen.

Into your hands I commit my spirit; redeem me, O LORD, the God of truth. (Psalm 31:5)

SAFE IN GOD'S HANDS

With Thee, Lord, have I cast my lot;
O faithful God, forsake me not,
To Thee my soul commending.
Lord, be my Stay, Lead Thou the way
Now and when life is ending.

(TLH 524:6)

The words of our psalm verse and those of our hymn stanza are quite familiar to us, particularly these words of prayer: "Into your hands I commit my spirit"; for so spoke our Redeemer as he closed his life on the cross.

Many of the noblest saints of God have died with these same words upon their lips. When Johann Huss was on his way to the stake, there was stuck on his head a paper cap scrawled over with the picture of the devil; but he said with sure, calm faith: "Father, into your hands I commit my spirit!"

These words show us the manner in which death can and should be met by all of God's children. We may meet the king of terrors with confidence, with profound repose, for he is a vanquished enemy whose sting has been removed. Note well, that which gives us the confidence to pray: "Father, into your hands I commit my spirit," is this word and assurance of faith: "Redeem me, O Lord God of truth!"

Those who rest in the redemption of Christ are people who can confidently commit themselves body and soul into the hands of God. They know they are safe because they know they are saved. They cling to his promise: "Fear not, for I have redeemed you; I have summoned you by name; you are mine." They know they are secure for all eternity. They say with Paul: "The Spirit himself testifies with our spirit that we are God's children. Now if we are children, then we are heirs—heirs of God and co-heirs with Christ, if indeed we share in his sufferings in order that we may also share in his glory" (Romans 8:16,17). The future shall be one of perfect beauty and blessedness.

But should we use those words only in death? Should we not be committed to the hands of our father every day of our life? Should not every day be a day of self-surrender? Should not our being, our body, our soul, our all be committed to him who has asked us in his love: "Commit your way to the LORD; trust in him and he will do this." That surrender will mean safety and security, blessing and bliss for every day.

"So be it," then I say
With all my heart each day.
We, too, dear Lord, adore Thee,
We sing for joy before Thee.
Guide us while here we wander
Until we praise Thee yonder. Amen.

When the LORD brought back the captives to Zion, we were like men who dreamed. Our mouths were filled with laughter, our tongues with songs of joy. Then it was said among the nations, "The LORD has done great things for them." The LORD has done great things for us, and we are filled with joy. (Psalm 126:1-3)

HOME AT LAST

A scene in New York Harbor affects the feelings of Americans returning from far corners of the globe. Travelers have said that, as they caught sight of the Statue of Liberty, they were overcome with emotion. That lofty torch told of freedoms they had seen in no other land. The sight stirred their hearts and brought forth tears of joy.

God's people are like this. Our text describes the feelings of Old Testament people returning from captivity to their beloved Jerusalem. It was too good to be true! As captives in a far-off land, they had dreamed of this moment. For years the older ones had tried to remember the hills of Jerusalem. Children had heard stories of the homeland they had never seen. Their minds had pictured the old Temple, since destroyed, with its sacrifices, prayers and worship. How they longed to be back there.

Finally it came true. At last they were home. It was like a splendid dream. How good God was to bring them to these delightful scenes. As the longtime exiles trod the holy ground of their fathers, they laughed and shouted and joined their neighbors in grateful songs. They were home! God had brought them home.

Are we not exiles today? While we, as Christians, have our hearts fixed on things of heaven, yet we live in this world, this "Babylon" of sin, grief and death. This captivity is troublesome. It makes the believer in Jesus long for deliverance. And in due time, God has promised, the deliverance will come. When we are escorted by the angels into heaven, we will see an eternal homeland that is beyond our fondest dreams. We will understand fully why it was that Jesus was willing to have "laid on him the iniquity of us all." Jesus died under our sins that his believers might share with him the grand joys of heaven.

These joys are beyond description. When the believer passes through the black but harmless curtain of death and first lays eyes on heaven, he will think he is dreaming. He will wonder how such joys can exist. He will see, as he never fully saw on earth, the immense value of Jesus' blood and death. It was truly a great price which brought sinners the glories of heaven. He will never cease to marvel that these glories are all his, and for no works of his own. Yes, the world had once laughed at the Christian. But now it will be his turn to break into the joyous laughter and singing of eternity. His Lord will have brought him home at last.

Comfort us, O God, with your promises of heavenly joy. Give us patient hearts to bear ridicule and temptation as we await heaven, and even now let us laugh and sing that we have forgiveness in Jesus Christ. Amen.

God is our refuge and strength, an ever-present help in trouble. Therefore we will not fear, though the earth give way and the mountains fall into the heart of the sea, though its waters roar and foam and the mountains quake with their surging. Selah. (Psalm 46:1-3)

GOD IS A VERY PRESENT HELP

When Luther was about to appear before the church council at Worms, he prayed thus: "O God, Almighty God everlasting! How dreadful is the world! Behold how its mouth opens to swallow me up, and how small is my faith in Thee! . . . Oh! The weakness of the flesh and the power of Satan! If I am to depend upon any strength of this world—all is over. . . . The knell is struck. . . . O God! O Thou my God! Help me against all the wisdom of this world. Forsake me not, for the sake of Thy well-beloved Son, Jesus Christ, my defense, my buckler, and my stronghold."

While Luther sang with confidence, "We tremble not, we fear no ill," he always did so with full knowledge of how weak he was. He recognized his need for strengthening from the Lord, who "surrounds his people, as the mountains surround Jerusalem" (Psalm 125:2).

In the history of the old covenant men had been granted visions to bring out this fact that God rings his people with defense in every danger. The army of Benhadad, king of Syria, came and stood around Dothan, the city in which the man of God Elisha lived. He sought to get rid of the prophet, who had proved to be such a thorn in the flesh for him and his people. A great host of horses and chariots came by night and surrounded the city. It was most terrifying to the servant of Elisha when, upon rising that morning, he beheld that very imposing army around the entire city. He rushed in to his master and said, "Oh, my lord, what shall we do?" "Don't be afraid," the prophet answered. "Those who are with us are more than those who are with them."

Elisha had the confidence that the Lord gives. But since the servant still lacked it, Elisha prayed, "O Lord, open his eyes so he may see." The Lord opened the eyes of the young man, and he saw the mountain full of horses and chariots of fire round about Elisha. God is a very present help, if men will only see him!

With might of ours can naught be done,
Soon were our loss effected;
But for us fights the Valiant One,
Whom God Himself elected.
Ask ye, Who is this? Jesus Christ it is,
Of Sabaoth Lord,
And there's none other God;
He holds the field forever.

(LH 262:2)

O Lord, who gives power to the faint and increases strength to those who have no might, help us, who are your children by faith in your Son, to know assuredly that no evil will befall us and that no plague can come nigh our dwelling. Amen.

The LORD . . . keep you; (Numbers 6:24)

KEPT IN HIS CARE

Now I lay me down to sleep;
I pray the Lord my soul to keep.
If I should die before I wake,
Take me to heaven for Jesus' sake.

We wonder how many thousands of children have learned that verse as their first bedtime prayer. And it's a good prayer. It reminds children, and their parents, that the Lord will keep them. They are in his care. The word translated "keep" in the Aaronic blessing says the same thing. Sometimes the Hebrew word is translated "guard" or "watch over." When God keeps us that is what he is doing— guarding us and watching over us.

Even when we are asleep, God is taking care of us. As one of the psalms says, "He who watches over you . . . will neither slumber nor sleep." In addition to his personal care, our loving God also uses his angels to keep us. Another psalm states this truth: "He will command his angels concerning you to guard you in all your ways."

What greater confidence could we ask for? The almighty God and his powerful angels are keeping us day and night. Many times without our realizing it they are keeping us from death or disaster on the highway. They keep us safe at home, at school and at work. More importantly, the Lord keeps us spiritually. Through his Word he keeps our faith alive and prevents us from falling into unbelief and eternal death.

This doesn't mean that we never have any troubles or heartaches. God says we can expect that while we live in this world. But because we are kept in his care, we know that everything is working together for our eternal good.

So even in the darkest hour we can be sure that God is keeping us. Even in the hour of death we know that he will keep us from falling away and will take us to heaven for Jesus' sake.

Because God is so good to us, there is something we will want to do for him. To show our love for him we will want to keep his commandments. That's our way of saying, "Thanks, Lord, for keeping me in your care!"

Hold Thou Thy Cross before my closing eyes,
Shine through the gloom, and point me to the skies.
Heaven's morning breaks, and earth's vain shadows flee;
In life, in death, O Lord, abide with me! Amen.

Then we your people, the sheep of your pasture, will praise you forever; from generation to generation we will recount your praise. (Psalm 79:13)

OUR TENDER SHEPHERD'S CARE

The shepherd guides his sheep along a narrow, stony path. Ever so often a sheep strays from the path to be brought back by a smarting blow of the shepherd's staff. Another straggles behind and would be lost, did not his shepherd poke him along. One slips off the mountain path and is caught on a ledge. The shepherd tenderly hauls him to safety with the crook of his staff. Even when the flock reaches the grass-covered slope of the valley, some are not satisfied, but stray from the rest only to expose themselves to the clutches of wild animals. These the shepherd seeks out, rescues and many a time nurses back to health. He is not content unless he can bring each one back to the safety of the fold.

We are such sheep of our Good Shepherd. Having made us his own through his holy, precious blood and innocent suffering and death, he leads us gently along the narrow and often forbidding pathway of life. Though we hesitate to follow, his voice continues to call and encourage, and to keep us from becoming lost. When we straggle behind, when we choose a more inviting byway of the world, when we stumble and fall into sin, his voice lovingly calls us back. At times his rod strikes very hard, but no matter from what depths of despair we cry out, we hear the voice of him who promises: "I will never leave you or forsake you." "Come, follow me!" We are delivered from all the hurts of sin by him who came to heal the broken-hearted and bind up their wounds. Our repentance and faith are always and continually answered by his Shepherd's care.

"So we your people and sheep of your pasture will praise you forever." In the same breath that we penitently pray with the psalmist: "Oh, do not hold against us our former iniquities," we are able to thank him for his goodness. He is so close to us with his saving Word that forgiveness and help are assured. So deep and heartfelt should be our gratitude that it cannot be kept hidden. As it has come down to us through the ages of our Lord's eternal grace, so is it ours to share from one generation to the next: "From generation to generation we will recount your praise."

O faithful Savior, we praise you for tenderly watching over your sheep; keep your eyes upon us when we are in danger of growing secure and careless; make us to see the weakness and helplessness of the flesh, and warn us to watch and pray that we may not put our trust in ourselves, but in fervent prayer call on you for help. Amen.

Since you are my rock and my fortress, for the sake of your name lead and guide me. (Psalm 31:3)

ONE PLUS GOD!

Thou art my Strength,
  my Shield, my Rock,
My Fortress that withstands each shock,
  My Help, my Life, my Treasure.
Whate'er the rod, Thou art my God;
  Naught can resist Thy pleasure.
(TLH 524:4)

No matter how great the danger or how mighty the foe, "if God be for us, who can be against us?" This truth is also expressed by the hymn stanza above. We *are* surrounded by fearsome foes and deadly dangers. We must not be unmindful of the fact that our "enemy the devil prowls around like a roaring lion looking for someone to devour." Make no mistake about it—he is a powerful foe. He comes with signs and lying wonders. He, too, could turn the Egyptian sorcerers' rods into serpents; he, too, could change Egypt's water into blood; he, too, could call up Samuel's spirit against Saul. He caused the hounding and harassment of David, and he causes the same for us. It is his evil will and counsel that seeks to hinder and hamper the good will of God. He is truly the old evil Foe!

Powerful he is, but not all-powerful. When he pitted his strength against God in heaven, he was defeated and cast out into hell. Now, God is our God, and when we say with David: "You are my God," we are saying that he is our Strength, our Fortress, our Help, our Life, our Treasure, our Shield and our Rock.

You may be only one; you may be all alone; you may be forsaken by all others; yet you are a majority with God. Surely, David experienced this truth in a most extraordinary way, when God sent him out to battle against the giant Goliath. Humanly speaking, David didn't have a ghost of a chance; but he was not alone; God's promise was behind him! One plus God is always a majority!

Paul Gerhardt has said it for us:

If God Himself be for me,
I may a host defy;
For when I pray, before me
My foes, confounded, fly.
If Christ, my Head and Master,
Befriend me from above,
What foe or what disaster
Can drive me from His love?
(TLH 528:1)

Why are we often so quick to forget and so slow to remember the power and promise of our God? Why are our fears so large and our faith so little? Why not build and bolster our faith with the power of his Word and rest securely and serenely on his promises? Is it mere idle talk when God says: "Commit your way to the LORD; trust in him and he will do this"? No; our trust shall ever be: "Thou art my rock and my fortress." "What'er the rod, Thou art my God; naught can resist thy pleasure."

I am trusting Thee for power;
Thine can never fail.
Words which Thou Thyself shalt give me
Must prevail. Amen.

But the men who had gone up with him said, "We can't attack those people; they are stronger than we are." And they spread among the Israelites a bad report about the land they had explored. They said, "The land we explored devours those living in it. All the people we saw there are of great size. We saw the Nephilim there (the descendants of Anak come from the Nephilim). We seemed like grasshoppers in our own eyes, and we looked the same to them." (Numbers 13:31-33)

THE FEAR OF FAILURE

It was a golden moment for the children of Israel. It was a time to take advantage of one of the opportunities the Lord was placing before them. After a long journey through the desert they had now come to the Promised Land. In obedience to a command of the Lord they sent spies to scout the land.

The resulting report was partly favorable. It spoke of a fruitful country; it pictured a land flowing with milk and honey. But the report was also partly unfavorable. A majority of the scouts emphasized the fortified town and formidable enemies they had seen; they were afraid.

They were afraid in spite of the Lord's promise to them. As Joshua and Caleb stated in a minority report, "If the Lord is pleased with us, he will lead us into that land. . . . The Lord is with us. Do not be afraid of them" (Numbers 14:8,9).

The problem that the majority of the scouts thought confronted them in the land of Canaan reflects a problem that frequently arises in the lives of all Christians. The fear of failure looms large.

To be sure, Christians are to count the cost before they embark on some venture. But that cost is to be counted in the light of the Lord's will. If we are confident that we are doing his will, then the fear of possible problems and fear that we might not succeed should not deter us. If we rely entirely on ourselves, we have a right to be fearful of the outcome. But if we are doing what the Lord wishes, then we can be assured that he will be with us in what we do.

This does not eliminate the possibility of problems, but it does remove the threat of failure. Troubles may well arise, but the final, *eternal* result will be success—even if, for the time being, we experience what appears to be nothing but pure failure and frustration. When Christ is with us, there are no ultimate failures or tragedies. Knowing that, let us move forward in faith and work during the daylight the Lord has given to us.

O Lord, give us the courage to take advantage of the opportunities that you place before us, and not to shrink in fear of failure. Amen.

And Abram said, "You have given me no children; so a servant in my household will be my heir." Then the word of the LORD came to him: "This man will not be your heir, but a son coming from your own body will be your heir." He took him outside and said, "Look up at the heavens and count the stars—if indeed you can count them." Then he said to him, "So shall your offspring be." (Genesis 15:3-5)

COUNT YOUR BLESSINGS

Astronomers have long ago given up trying to count the stars. With entire galaxies thought to be still undiscovered, who can say how many stars there are? Counting the stars is an impossibility. It must be put into the same category as walking on the ceiling, burning water on the stove or lifting oneself up by his own bootstraps. It cannot be done.

What then could Abram hope to accomplish by trying to count the stars? For one thing, he might begin to see how wrong he was. Today when a person has made an error of judgment, we say that he was "off by a mile." Abram was off more than that. How badly he had miscalculated his future! How foolish he was to doubt God's promise and God's ability! He had begun to doubt that God was able to give him one offspring, but God was going to give him as many as the stars. Therefore as he counted the stars, the sheer multitude of those stars was a gentle reminder to Abram how far wrong he had been in doubting God.

But every one of those twinkling stars also represented a blessing from God to Abram. In counting the stars, Abram was at the same time counting his blessings from God. Every star was a sign of God's love and faithfulness. God would keep his word. He would give Abram offspring as numerous as the stars, just as he had promised.

Today the stars still twinkle in the heavens to remind us how wrong anyone would be who doubted God. Just as the rainbow stands in the heavens as an assurance of God's faithfulness, so the stars are witnesses of that same great faithfulness. When we see the stars and think of Abram's blessings, we might also think of our own blessings. Our blessings too are as numerous as the stars.

Take time out this evening. If weather permits, go outside and count the stars. Count your blessings if you can. What a wonderful God we have! How great and how good! What God is able to give, man cannot count—blessings as many as the stars.

Thank you, Lord, for all your blessings to me. They are as many as the stars. Thank you especially for my Savior. Amen.

"Yet I reserve seven thousand in Israel—all whose knees have not bowed down to Baal and all whose mouths have not kissed him." (1 Kings 19:18)

WE ARE NOT ALONE

Loneliness is a problem which everyone faces at sometime in their life. It has been known to lead a person to drink, to commit suicide, to have an extramarital affair, to even lose one's sanity. It might even be safe to say that loneliness leads to no good, because it so often leads to despair.

Despair can be unbearable. The devil would have us believe that we are all alone because of our sins. He plants thoughts in our minds such as: "God can't possibly forgive you for that. Don't listen to all that bunk about not having to do anything to make up for your shortcomings. You can work it out yourself." This kind of thinking led Martin Luther to try to work out his own peace with God. In the process he nearly killed himself.Our sinful minds can also come up with ideas about despair. "What's the use of living, no one loves me!" "I can't have this baby now; it will destroy my career." Elijah, prophet of God, was just as good at despairing as we are. "I am the only one left; take my life," he told God.

Certainly each of us has problems. They may seem unbearable, and we just cannot cope with them. As Christians, however, we have been given a joy that is greater than any of the problems we have now or ever will have. Our joy is found in our Savior who has rescued us from the clutches of sin by his death on the cross. He has rescued us from the power of death by his resurrection. He continues to rescue us every day from problems, despair and temptation by being with us. Through his Word he continues to come to us with the reassurance that we are not alone in our fight against sin, death and the devil. The sweet message of his gospel turns our sorrow over sin into joy and expectation. The hope of heaven is ours.

This hope of heaven is something we have in common with our fellow Christians. Just as the Lord needed to remind Elijah that the church still existed, so we too need to hear that we are not alone. We have fellow sufferers in Christ. God's Word and his church will endure forever.

Thank you, Lord Jesus, for coming to this earth to share in our suffering. Keep the joys of heaven before us at all times, lest we allow sin to lead us to despair. Amen.

The LORD will watch over your coming and going both now and forevermore. (Psalm 121:8)

BLESS OUR GOING OUT WE PRAY

How has everything gone so far today? Did it turn out just as you expected it would? Or were there some surprises? Some disappointments? Did you please God in all your thoughts and desires, your words and deeds? Or did you sin?

However things went for you this day, you've made it through only because God walked with you. He provided for all your needs. He preserved and protected you in all your ways. He blessed your coming into today, your journey through it, and now also your going out of it.

As Christians we surely know that we have good reason to be thankful for each day of our lives. Because of our sinfulness, we have deserved nothing good from God. It is only because of Jesus, our Savior, that God has been with us and blessed us so bountifully. It is because of God's mercy in Christ that we were not consumed by his anger. He has rather granted us his peace and love, pardon and protection.

At the end of each day, each week, and at the end of our lives, we can fall asleep and rest in peace. God has preserved our coming in and will also preserve our going out according to his promises. By faith in Christ I know that he has forgiven me all my sins and will graciously keep me this night. Into his hands, I can commend my body and soul and all things. His holy angels will be with me that the wicked Foe may have no power over me.

We have walked with God today. We entered it in his name, bringing him our sorrows and needs, our worries and sins. He has met us right here through his living Word and bestowed upon us all the blessings of salvation. What faith and joy, courage and strength are ours in Jesus Christ.

May we spend every day and every week walking with God in worship and prayer. Then he will indeed bless us and keep us. He will make his face shine upon us and be gracious unto us. He will lift up his countenance upon us and give us peace.

Bless our going out, we pray, bless our entrance in like measure; bless our bread, O Lord, each day, bless our toil, our rest, our pleasure; bless us when we reach death's portal, bless us then with life immortal. Amen.

As the deer pants for streams of water, so my soul pants for you, O God. My soul thirsts for God, for the living God. When can I go and meet with God? My tears have been my food day and night, while men say to me all day long, "Where is your God?" These things I remember as I pour out my soul: how I used to go with the multitude, leading the procession to the house of God, with shouts of joy and thanksgiving among the festive throng. Why are you downcast, O my soul? Why so disturbed within me? Put your hope in God, for I will yet praise him, my Savior and my God. (Psalm 42:1-5)

THE CRY OF THE SOUL HOMESICK FOR GOD

Have you ever been homesick? There are those who make fun of this sickness as though it were a mere childish weakness. But men with really broad shoulders have this sickness.

The author whom God inspired to write Psalm 42 was homesick. His homesickness, however, had this peculiarity that he was depressed, not because of his absence from home, but because of his absence from God's house and from fellow worshipers in that house. The son of Korah who wrote this psalm appears to have been in exile with David at the time when the king had to flee before his son Absalom. So he found himself surrounded by heathen people who constantly made fun of him because of his religion. They were always trying to make a fool out of him because of his childlike trust in his God. How this man would have loved to run away from the taunting unbelievers and again enjoy religious services with God's people! But at the moment that privilege was not his. That made him homesick.

Have you ever been homesick for God and for the church service? If you have been in a situation where you could not enjoy your accustomed church service, then you will have had this homesickness. Christians simply cannot escape such homesickness for God and for his house. For every soul that knows God feels its need for him very keenly. Where there is no feeling or real need for God, there Christianity has ceased to exist. Only God can give that spiritual life which is known as Christianity, and only God can sustain it. He does so through his Word and sacraments. The Christian realizes that when he is cut off from the Word and sacrament, his Christianity is in danger. For that reason he experiences the pangs of homesickness when he cannot enjoy the Means of Grace regularly in the public service.

Most of us are not cut off from public worship. Do we cherish this blessing?

Heavenly Father, graciously give us hearts that would be homesick for you and your house if we lacked the privilege of regular worship there. We ask this in Jesus' name. Amen.

Can a mother forget the baby at her breast and have no compassion on the child she has borne? (Isaiah 49:15)

GOD'S GRACIOUS CONCERN FOR HIS PEOPLE

The people of God in Isaiah's time had questioned God's concern for his chosen ones. Likewise, in the hour of despair when our faith becomes weak, we are in need of God's strengthening Word of assurance. Though it may seem to us that we are forgotten and forsaken, yet God would have us put such thoughts out of mind by asking us to contemplate the question, "Can a mother forget the baby at her breast and have no compassion on the child she has borne?"

Luther, in his commentary on this text, presents some beautiful thoughts for our consideration: "The love of a mother's heart cannot forget its child. This is unnatural. A woman would be ready to go through fire for her children. So you see how hard women labor in cherishing, feeding and watching. To this emotion God compares himself, as if to say, 'I will not forsake you, because I am your mother. I cannot desert you.' In that word there is comprised the example of a woman, and from it we derive our consolation."

The second question that God asks his children as he puts their faith to the test is, "Can a mother . . . have no compassion on the child she has borne?" The word "compassion" in this text suggests a very close tie—like that which exists between a mother and her beloved son. She is ready to make sacrifices for her son even though they may not be noticed or appreciated. She is willing to forgive him when he has done wrong. She is willing to forget ingratitude. She is ready to show mercy even when the son's behavior causes feelings of frustration and disappointment.

Our God here uses the example of what is most likely the greatest of human loves—that of a mother for her infant child. Yet even this love will change because of sinful human nature. The daily papers regularly carry the news of parents abandoning or abusing their children. Usually the children are not to blame.

Our heavenly Father is not like a human parent. Because of our sin he could abandon us to a fate worse than death—eternal death. Instead he sent his Son to take our punishment and die our death. For Jesus' sake God forgives us all our sins. He is most graciously concerned about our eternal welfare.

Lord God, heavenly Father, continue to manifest your love and forgiveness to us. We believe that your love is greater than that of any mother, for you gave your Son for our salvation. Amen.

The LORD has done this, and it is marvelous in our eyes. This is the day the LORD has made; let us rejoice and be glad in it. (Psalm 118:23,24)

A DAY NOT TO BE FORGOTTEN

Whenever we have experienced a day of special significance or joy, it is not easily forgotten. We never really tire of thinking about it or talking of it. It is even more so with this day which the Lord has made, the day of our Lord's triumphant resurrection from the dead. When we truly realize the tremendous significance of that day for the Lord Jesus and for ourselves, we understand that this day is not one to be soon forgotten.

The blessings of Easter are meant for us to enjoy each day of our lives. This day, then, ought to remain great and marvelous in our eyes at all times.

Certainly, we then will never tire of hearing the message of what God has done for us in raising Jesus from the dead. God wants us to live each day with faith in the risen Christ and with the eternal hope that he has made sure for us. Each day we have work to do for our Lord; there are new problems in life to face and overcome, new responsibilities to carry out.

Let Easter give constant strength, courage and confidence to our faith. It reminds us that we have a risen and living Lord who cares for us, who provides for all our needs, who helps us do all things, who lives to forgive our sins daily and bless us with peace in our hearts.

When we may have the sad duty to stand at the open grave of a believing loved one, let us again remember this day which the Lord has made, this day of our Lord's victory over death and the grave. Our tears will dry as we hear him say to us: "For the perishable must clothe itself with the imperishable, and the mortal with immortality."

Scripture reminds us that we were buried with Christ by baptism into death, that like as he was raised up from the dead by the glory of the Father, even so we should walk in newness of life. We were once dead in sin and under Satan's tyranny. But Christ has redeemed us from all that. He paid the price. We have risen with him to a new life. Let the day of Easter remain marvelous in our eyes in this way, too, that we walk in a new life. Let us daily crucify the flesh with its affections and lusts, growing in love, and all good works, living under Christ in his kingdom, and rejoicing in hope.

Finally, when we ourselves must go down to the grave, let us hold firmly the hand of our victorious Savior. Our hearts will then be comforted, knowing that we shall ever be with the Lord.

Grant me grace, O blessed Savior,
And Thy Holy Spirit send
That my walk and my behavior
May be pleasing to the end;
That I may not fall again
Into Death's grim pit and pain,
Whence by grace Thou hast retrieved me
And from which Thou hast relieved me. Amen.

"This is what the LORD says—your Redeemer, who formed you in the womb: 'I am the LORD, who has made all things, who alone stretched out the heavens, who spread out the earth by myself.' " (Isaiah 44:24)

OUR LIFE IS SECURE FOR ETERNITY

Life is such a struggle. We never know from one moment to the next what to expect. Of one thing we Christians can be sure, and that is that, "We must go through many hardships to enter the kingdom of God" (Acts 14:22). Satan would have a field day with this truth. He causes our sinful nature to focus on the "hardships." Our old Adam doesn't like hardships. It likes ease and pleasure. Satan likes to whisper in our ears, "See, God wants you to suffer."

This is when we need God's reminder that he is our Redeemer. He called us to be his own people even before the world itself was formed. Having been made and redeemed by God himself, we can answer Satan's objection with, "hardships, yes, to enter God's kingdom."

Trials and tribulations will come our way. It often seems as though we Christians have more trials than anyone else. Yet God has prepared for us an eternity of glory. With such a prospect before us we can see our trials as only temporary, and as means by which God readies us for heaven.

God also reminds us of his almighty power. By his power he made all things. What we can see, as well as what we cannot see, came into existence when God said, "Let there be!" The wondrous heavens above and the beautiful earth beneath exist because God made them and preserves them. God also emphasizes that he did this alone.

This almighty God is the God who loves us with an everlasting love. He sent his only-begotten Son "that whoever believes in him shall not perish but have eternal life."

He forgives us all our sins, creating in us faith which trusts in Jesus alone as Lord and Savior. He made us what we are. We are his sheep and lambs, who rest in his almighty, loving hands.

"If God is for us, who can be against us? He who did not spare his own Son, but gave him up for us all—how will he not also, along with him, graciously give us all things?" (Romans 8:31-32) Having redeemed us by Jesus' death, he lets us know that our lives are secure for eternity by Jesus' resurrection.

Lord God, by your almighty power graciously keep us secure from all harm and danger unto eternal life, for Jesus' sake. Amen.

"Have I not commanded you? Be strong and courageous. Do not be terrified; do not be discouraged, for the LORD your God will be with you wherever you go." (Joshua 1:9)

GO WITH GOD

Once before the children of Israel had been up to the Promised Land. Fear had kept them out. Yes, it was a land flowing with milk and honey. But there were difficulties in taking it. The people who lived there were very strong, and their cities were protected with stout walls. So the children of Israel were afraid to try to go in. God had promised that he would give them the land, but they were not willing to take him at his word. Theirs was a fear born of unbelief.

Unbelief still produces fear. Unbelief can paralyze our mission program if we are afraid to go out and possess the land for Christ. We may find all kinds of excuses for not carrying out God's commands, but the real reason is usually fear and unbelief.

That's why God still tells us in his Word, "Be strong and courageous. Do not be terrified; do not be discouraged, for the Lord your God will be with you wherever you go." The Lord takes care of us as we walk! He is our Good Shepherd, defending us with his strong rod, and guiding us with his staff. He is our Comforter and Protector in the valley of death. Wherever we go in faith, we can also go with confidence because he goes with us!

"Go with God, then." This was the message given to Joshua and the people of Israel. This is the message for us. Young people can "go with God," as they plan their education, their work and their life. Parents can "go with God" through all the difficulties along life's way. And those who are approaching the end of their journey can "go with God" even through death's dark valley.

God gave the land to Joshua and the faithful people of Israel. The forbidding walls of Jericho crumbled before the blast of their trumpets. The inhabitants of the land fled in fear before the army of God's people. "The Lord is with them and he fights for them," they cried.

Go with God and your goal is assured, a God-pleasing life here on earth and a glorious crown of life in heaven! Fear him, and you will have nothing else to fear, as he says,

"Fear not, I am with thee,
oh, be not dismayed;
For I am thy God and
will still give thee aid;
I'll strengthen thee, help thee,
and cause thee to stand,
Upheld by My righteous,
omnipotent hand!"

Lord, be with me, and I shall not be afraid! Amen.

The LORD . . . give you peace. (Numbers 6:26)

A LASTING PEACE

Just what is this peace God gives us? There is a little story which, I believe, precisely illustrates the peace of God. The story tells of an artist who was asked to paint a picture that would visualize the idea of peace. The artist painted a roaring waterfall with a large tree hanging over it. On a limb of that tree, bending over the churning waters and almost touched by the rising spray, a sparrow calmly sat on her nest. Amid the roar and danger of the waterfall, the tiny bird was at peace.

That is a picture of our peace from God. Like that bird, we are surrounded by danger and troubles. But in the middle of all life's turmoil the Lord gives us peace. We are at rest.

Jesus assures us, "Peace I leave with you; my peace I give you. Do not let your hearts be troubled and do not be afraid." Our hearts are at peace. We know that the almighty God loves us. We know that life's dangers can bring us no lasting harm. We know that the joys of heaven lie ahead. This is the peace, lasting peace, God leaves us.

It is not a peace that comes naturally. We had been God's enemies—at war with him, rebelling against his every command. But our sins have been washed away in the blood of Christ. The Holy Spirit has brought us to faith in Christ as our Savior. St. Paul put it this way, "Since we have been justified through faith, we have peace with God through our Lord Jesus Christ."

There's something else special about this peace. It's for each of us. Throughout the Aaronic blessing the original Hebrew language uses the singular for "you." God's peace is not just for "you" as a large group of people. It's for "you" as a priceless individual. You may be a parent or a child. You might live alone or in barracks or a dormitory with hundreds of other people. You might be a man or woman, black or white, living in America or across the seas. It doesn't matter; you can still have peace. God's peace is for you!

That means, of course, that others can also enjoy it. Share the peace you have. Confess your Savior. With your gifts and prayers support God's missionaries—those messengers of life and peace.

Grant us Thy peace throughout our earthly life,
Our Balm in sorrow and our Stay in strife;
Then, when Thy voice shall bid our conflict cease,
Call us, O Lord, to Thine eternal peace. Amen.

**"In those days Judah will be saved and Jerusalem will live in safety."
(Jeremiah 33:16)**

THE CHRISTIAN'S SAFETY NET

A construction company in charge of building a bridge across a rather large body of water discovered that by putting a net below the men working on the steel girders of the bridge the efficiency and attitude of the workers rose dramatically. Just knowing that there was a net below to keep them from drowning gave the men a confidence and sense of security that they just couldn't have without it.

The sufferings and death of our Lord Jesus Christ have the same effect on us spiritually. God told the children of Israel that when the promised Messiah, the righteous Branch from David's line, would come, Judah would be saved and Jerusalem would live in safety. God was not simply referring to a time of earthly peace for Israel during the years that Jesus walked on this earth. He was referring to that peace which surpasses all understanding. That peace comes from a knowledge of the forgiveness of all our sins in Christ. By shedding his holy, precious blood on the cross and suffering its pain and torment, Jesus paid in full the penalty for all our sins. Because of Jesus' death on the cross we do not have to fear death. We do not have to fear judgment day, for neither death nor hell can harm us. Because of Jesus' death on the cross for our sins there is peace once more between God and man.

The knowledge of forgiveness in Christ, the knowledge that come what may, we are safe from eternal death and damnation, gives us as believers in Christ a peace, a confidence and a sense of security that sickness or sorrow, hardship or trouble, pain or even death cannot shake. The Apostle Paul states it so beautifully, "For I am convinced that neither death nor life, neither angels nor demons, neither the present nor the future, nor any powers, neither height nor depth, nor anything else in all creation, will be able to separate us from the love of God that is in Christ Jesus our Lord."

Peace in our hearts, confidence to face any situation in life, and a sure hope of eternal life in heaven some day are the "net" results of Jesus' suffering and death on the cross. May the cross of Jesus Christ be ever before our eyes throughout our life.

O loving Father, may the cross of Christ calm all our fears and give us peace and hope all the days of our life here on earth. Amen.

Though the fig tree does not bud and there are no grapes on the vines, though the olive crop fails and the fields produce no food, though there are no sheep in the pen and no cattle in the stalls, yet I will rejoice in the Lord, I will be joyful in God my Savior. (Habakkuk 3:17,18)

JOY WHEN YOU'RE DOWN AND OUT

"Good morning," said the man as he passed the stranger on the sidewalk. To his surprise the stranger turned and said, "I have never had a bad morning." "May you always be so fortunate," he replied. "I have never been unfortunate," the stranger said. "Then may you always be so happy." To that the stranger replied, "I've never been unhappy."

There probably are few people in the world who would answer as that stranger did—and fewer still who would think he was telling the truth. The prophet Habakkuk, however, seems to be speaking in this euphoric way in our devotional text. And he means what he says, because he knows the Lord is in charge and that all things serve the Lord's purpose. Habakkuk can say in his prayer that no matter what happens he will be joyful in the Lord.

Habakkuk paints a picture of perhaps the most desperate situation which people in Bible times could possibly envision. If there were no figs, grapes, olives, grain or domestic animals—items which were the very staples of life—it would be most difficult to survive.

When droughts came, people feared just such a thing. Apart from capture and death at the hands of their enemies they could imagine nothing worse.

Even if he were to be in such a desperate situation, Habakkuk says he would still rejoice in the Lord. Why? The words of Paul to the Romans, chapter 8, give the answer, "If God is for us who can be against us?" With God on our side we are never at a loss. The situation may seem desperate, even totally hopeless, but he who loved us so much that he sent his Son to die for our sins will take care of us and give us all we need.

Perhaps we will never experience a situation so desperate as that which Habakkuk describes, but sometimes money may be scarce, it may even be difficult to put food on the table. Even then we can rejoice in God our Savior, in whom we have forgiveness and eternal life in heaven. No one can ever take that away from us, and having that, we have everything—including the assurance that he will take adequate care of us during our life on earth.

Heavenly Father, you have taken care of our greatest need, our need for forgiveness and salvation in Jesus our Savior. Strengthen us in our convictions that you will take care of our other needs as well. Help us to rejoice in all circumstances. Amen.

Let the sea resound, and everything in it, the world, and all who live in it. Let the rivers clap their hands, let the mountains sing together for joy. (Psalm 98:7,8)

NOTHING BUT JOY AND THE SOUNDS OF JOY

It is difficult for us to visualize a life without sorrows, pains, tears and death. These are man's common experience here, and not man's only, but of all creatures since the fall into sin. Groaning and travail or anguish—how familiar! But how tragic, too, for those who believe that it is the only world that ever shall be!

It is precisely from the curse over this world that a gracious God has redeemed us. For those who accept this redemption and trust the precious promises of God there is a great comfort. They foresee by faith the new heaven and earth which God has prepared for them. In this new heaven and earth there is nothing but joy and the sounds of joy. The whole environment in this new life reflects and echoes the songs of praise and joy of God's redeemed people: The sea roars or thunders, the rivers clap their hands, the mountains sing together for joy.

Truly, "you have made known to me the path of life; you will fill me with joy in your presence, with eternal pleasures at your right hand."

Even in this life, in the hour of worship, as we hear God speak to us and so reveal his love again and again; as we are assured of forgiveness, peace and an inheritance with the saints in light, we have some small foretaste of the glorious reign of the Savior in the next world. We sense, and in a small way begin to understand and appreciate, the joys that shall be ours.

How this prospect of the eternal reign of Christ and the bliss it brings us stirs up feelings of hope and confidence! Though we may face sorrows and troubles here, they are eased and made light by him who calls us to himself to give us rest. Indeed, the sufferings of this present time are not worthy to be compared with the glory which shall be revealed in us.

With these wonderful and sure promises of God before us, with glimpses of the good things God has prepared for them that love him, we will hold fast in faith to the Savior Jesus Christ and patiently await the day that brings us nothing but joy.

Lord God, let us live and die in peace, for our eyes have seen your salvation in Christ, your Son and our Redeemer. Amen.

Praise the LORD, O my soul; all my inmost being, praise his holy name. Praise the LORD, O my soul, and forget not all his benefits—who forgives all your sins and heals all your diseases, who redeems your life from the pit and crowns you with love and compassion, who satisfies your desires with good things so that your youth is renewed like the eagle's. (Psalm 103:1-5)

PRAISE THE LORD, O MY SOUL

S oar like an eagle! Who can soar like an eagle? The true Christian can! For he has been born again to a "lively hope" through the Gospel of God.

In olden times the eagle had a reputation for quick recovery and the ability to make a fresh start, with energy, wings and feathers renewed. And such also is the rebirth which the Holy Spirit accomplishes in God's people. That is why their jubilation and thanksgiving are not a sometime thing, but a way of life. "Praise the Lord, O my soul!"

Outside of Christ it is hard to think of life as a celebration of God's benefits. For the eye of reason surveys the ruin of human nature caused by the Fall: everywhere there is greed and strife, disease and death. Yes, even within ourselves we sense the corruption and weakness which come from sin. Deep in their hearts all men tremble at the ripening judgment of God the Holy One!

What, then, is different about the Christian, that his heart alone brims over with praise to the Holy One? Nothing but the exceeding charity of God in Christ. For through Jesus Christ God has bought our lives back from damnation and eternal death. God has satisfied his justice with that one precious death upon Calvary's cross—there need be no more. The Christian lives in this truth.

Now if God's love is the great, active reality in my heart, then all of life wears a new face. There is healing when I need it and ask for it, in order that I may live and praise the works of the Lord. There are good gifts at every turn: parents, spouse, family, friends, food, shelter, the air, the earth, the land I love. Even hardship and heartache become forms of grace when I think about God's tender care. And at the last, the crown of eternal life! "Praise the Lord, O my soul, and forget not all his benefits!"

I will sing my Maker's praises
And in Him most joyful be,
For in all things I see traces
Of His tender love to me. . . .
All things else have but their day,
God's great love abides for aye. Amen.

You will go out in joy and be led forth in peace; the mountains and hills will burst into song before you, and all the trees of the field will clap their hands. (Isaiah 55:12)

FOLLOWING WHERE GOD LEADS

The final blessing of the Christian faith is to depart from this world in peace and to enter into everlasting glory. Christ makes our death a glorious victory rather than a final defeat. From that moment on our joy is complete.

The whole Bible prepares us for that moment of triumph. When Adam and Eve left the Garden of Eden, they took God's gracious promise of redemption with them. The blessings that they lost in Eden would ultimately be restored to them when they would leave this sin-infected world. The Exodus from Egypt reminds us how God will deliver us from the bondage of sin and bring us into the heavenly land of promise. We find the same reassurance in the return of the Jews from 70 years of exile in Babylon. Jesus promises, "I am going there to prepare a place for you. And if I go and prepare a place for you, I will come back and take you to be with me" (John 14:2,3). So we know where we are going as we follow Jesus.

There will be no perfect outward joy or peace along the way. We can expect trouble and sorrow as long as we live in this world. We will experience our share of uncertainty and doubt, disappointment and failure. If we follow Jesus, we may expect the same kind of treatment as he received from this world. With the help of God, however, we can learn to rejoice even in our tribulations. We have God's promise that he will make all things work together for our good.

We are at peace with God through faith in Christ Jesus. Nothing destroys inner peace like a guilty conscience. As we do our best to follow the guidance of God's Word day by day, our consciences remain clear. As we daily receive God's forgiveness for our many misdeeds, we are at peace with God.

As we go on our way hand in hand with Jesus, as we faithfully follow his instructions, we need not worry at all. We are not responsible for the way that things finally turn out; he is. Our only duty is to follow and to obey. He assures us that we will finally reach the perfect joy and peace of our heavenly home.

In our final moment of triumph we may pray with pious Simeon:

Sovereign Lord, as you have promised, you now dismiss your servant in peace. For my eyes have seen your salvation, which you have prepared in the sight of all people. Amen.

Even to your old age and gray hairs I am he, I am he who will sustain you. I have made you and I will carry you; I will sustain you and I will rescue you. (Isaiah 46:4)

OUR ONE AND ONLY SOURCE OF SECURITY

Many people in the world today are desperately searching for security—security from the cradle to the grave. In their minds, if they could find the right combination of material blessings, such as the perfect job with high pay and a solid retirement plan, they would never need to worry again. If they would only look around them and consider what has happened to others like them who have placed their trust and sought their security in the things of this world! There is no lasting security in the material things of life.

What these worldly minded people are doing is little different from what God's ancient people, Israel, had done. Israel turned away from God and sought security, peace of mind, in things of this world. People today make money, a good position, earthly goods, their gods. They are thus caught up in various forms of idolatry. But their search for security in such false gods of this world is useless and vain.

In our portion of God's Word, the Lord reminds Israel that he is their one and only source of true security. He reminds them of the loving care he has shown them in the past, saying, "I have made and I will carry you; even I will sustain . . . you." It is the Lord God of Israel who had created them and had cared for them in their youth. He is the One who was providing for them now and would continue to do so even unto their old age. "Even to your old age . . . I am he," is God's assurance.

What God is saying here applies also to us. He is our faithful God who has provided for us in the past, is doing so now, and will continue to provide for us all the days of our life. Our faithful God provides all the security we need in this world. He also provides for our eternal life. This is what he means when he says in the final words of our text, ". . . and (I) will rescue you."

The psalmist, by God's inspiration, reassures us of these same wondrous blessings, saying, "The Lord will watch over your coming and going both now and forevermore" (Psalm 121:8). Our faithful God is our God from eternity to eternity.

Lord, we thank you for your promises to preserve us for evermore for Jesus' sake. Amen.

In you our fathers put their trust; they trusted and you delivered them. (Psalm 22:4)

WHOM DO YOU TRUST?

We can't live without trust. Marriage is a relationship based on mutual trust. Children trust and depend on their parents. Patients who submit to surgery rely on the doctor's skilled hands.

But on earth our confidence is often misplaced, often disappointed. We trust our physical strength, yet illness lays us low. We build our assets with investments, and then a recession comes to threaten our security. We trust friends with secrets only to find their hearts are false and that they use their tongues against us. We trust our own opinions, only to find that they often don't square with facts.

Our ideals lie shattered, our goals unattained, our ambitions unfulfilled. In the end we find that self-reliance is able to produce nothing but depression and despair.

The psalmist reminds us to redirect our trust and to focus our attention on God, who alone is trustworthy. We can rely on him because we have proof that he has acted mightily for us. In Jesus Christ God assumed the burden of our broken nature and canceled out the charge of sin. By his death and resurrection Jesus demonstrated that the God of power is the God of love who is "for us." He is the same powerful God who again and again delivered his people down through the ages.

On earth there is no sure and snappy cure for all that ails us. There is no insurance policy that will protect us against illness and death. Neither does God tell us in his Word that we will have a heaven on earth. Our calling as Christians is not to sit back and drink in the pleasures of this world, but to toil and labor while it is day—to seek the welfare of Christ's kingdom. This is not without suffering and trouble. We are still sinners living in a world that is under God's curse. But he has promised his presence even in the middle of toil and trouble, crisis and calamity. He sustains us through sorrow and strengthens us through strife with a grace that is sufficient for us. He protects us and delivers us from all that would harm us or rob us of our salvation. And in the end he will bring us into heaven, where we will find our eternal rest and joy in him.

Lord God, you have always proved faithful to your promises in the past. Our fathers will agree that you have blessed them in every way. We know from your Word that you will fulfill all your promises to us now and in the future. Keep us safe in the hollow of your hand, for the sake of your Son, Jesus Christ. We have put our trust in you. Amen.

And the LORD **commanded the fish, and it vomited Jonah onto dry land. (Jonah 2:10)**

DO HEROES NEED HELP?

"**I** had a lot of help along the way." True heroes in whatever walk of life will gladly admit to this. They will readily speak of the help given to them by a father or mother, a teacher, a coach, a husband or wife, or a friend. How many an award of achievement has not been accepted accompanied by the words, "I would like to recognize and thank those who helped me."

As Jonah lay on the dry land along the seashore, he might well have sighed within his heart, "I would like to recognize and thank him who helped me." Jonah had not done a thing to help himself. But help came. It came from God. The Lord, who controls all things in his creation, told that large fish to spit Jonah out, and out came Jonah. All of nature bows to the mighty commands of its Creator. Neither did Jonah have to do the rest on his own. There was no distance to shore he still had to swim. He was placed directly and safely on dry land. Jonah did nothing but trust his Lord. And the Lord helped!

"I'll do it myself," is often the contention of the little child learning the skills of life. And often frustration results because he has not yet learned the value of needing and accepting help. Needing help, accepting help, and recognizing help with appreciation after it is given are not signs of weakness. This is wisdom and experience showing up. In the Christian, it is also evidence of faith.

"My help comes from the LORD, the Maker of heaven and earth" (Psalm 121:2). How ready, willing and happy we are to admit this at all times, even as we do in the service each time we go to God's house. We look to our past with all of its ups and downs, its sicknesses and worries, its sorrows and heartaches, and its joys and accomplishments; and, behold, we made it through them all.

As people of faith, by the grace of God, we are not at all ashamed to admit, in fact, we declare it loudly, "I had a lot of help along the way." God was our help in the past. And that gives foundation to our confidence that he will continue to be our help in the days to come. Correctly, we look to the future with the words, "The Lord is my helper; I will not be afraid. What can man do to me?" (Hebrews 13:6) That is not a cry of weakness. That is a hero talking—a hero of faith.

Dear Father, even as you have helped me in the past, graciously help me in the days to come. Amen.

Then you will call, and the LORD will answer; you will cry for help, and he will say: "Here am I." (Isaiah 58:9)

THE BLESSED PRIVILEGE OF PRAYER

"What a privilege to carry ev'rything to God in prayer!" The words of the familiar hymn express well the importance which Christians attach to prayer. It is a wonderful privilege that we are able to speak to God in prayer. It is a privilege to be able to call upon him and to know that he will answer. It is a privilege to be able to cry to him in time of need and to know that he will respond with an almighty, "Here I am."

People often forget that prayer is a privilege granted only to believers. Only the repentant have access to God through prayer. No one else has that privilege—not the person who refuses to admit his sins, nor the person who depends on himself for salvation, nor the Buddhist, nor the Hindu, nor anyone who looks for salvation elsewhere than in the life and death of Jesus.

Failure to repent closes the door in Jesus' face. We must remember that a closed door does not allow passage in or out. Not only does the closed door of the unrepentant heart shut Jesus out, that same door prevents a person from going to the Father in prayer.

Failure to repent can only be called a tragedy. It deprives a person of all the blessings of salvation. That person is without the privilege of prayer. That person has shut the door to God's saving presence.

What a privilege prayer is for us! How wonderful to have access to the Lord! A long line of believers can be called upon to testify to the power of prayer. Moses requested, "I beseech Thee," and God answered his request. Samuel sought God's help against the Philistines. Help was provided. Elijah prayed for fire on Mt. Carmel. Fire poured down from heaven. The mighty power of a prayer-answering God is the only explanation for Daniel's deliverance from the lions' den. While in the fish's belly, Jonah repented and called upon the Lord. The Lord rescued him. Peter was released from prison at the request of Christians who prayed without ceasing.

If prayer was an exercised privilege in the lives of Moses, Samuel, Elijah, Daniel, Jonah, Peter and countless others, prayer can be an equally blessed privilege in our lives as repentant and believing Christians.

Lord, give me a repentant heart and hear and answer my prayers for Jesus' sake. Amen.

Abraham remained standing before the LORD. Then Abraham spoke up . . . "I have been so bold as to speak to the LORD, though I am nothing but dust and ashes." (Genesis 18:22,27)

GREAT AND SMALL, TAKE THEM ALL TO THE LORD

"There is a time for everything, and a season for every activity under heaven . . . a time to be silent and a time to speak" (Ecclesiastes 3:1,7). There are times when we stand silent before the Lord. We want him to speak to us. It may be at church or at home. When God speaks to us in his Word it is time to listen. What God has to tell us is important.

There are other times when we have the need to speak to our Father in heaven. It makes sense to go to him in prayer. His power has no limits. His love knows no bounds. Whatever our burden, we can turn it over to the One who is willing to carry it for us. We can place on his shoulders those concerns which are so small we hesitate to bring them up.

And what about big problems? God will solve them too—not only our worries about physical health or earthly losses, but also our concerns about sin, the weakness of our faith, our hot-and-cold attitude toward his Word and sacraments.

Our problems great and small we take to the Lord in prayer.

Abraham here serves as a fine example for us.

Abraham's words above, "I am nothing but dust and ashes," are well spoken. The words express humility. They remind us that we who are sinners, blind, dead and enemies of God by nature need to approach him on our knees. We are never disappointed when we plead for mercy. It is through our Savior that we have access to God. Jesus Christ has redeemed us from all sins, from death and from the power of the devil. Therefore we can come boldly to the Lord and make our requests known to him.

Yes, we approach God humbly, boldly and fully persuaded that he will hear and answer us. The Apostle Paul says reassuringly, "He who did not spare his own Son, but gave him up for us all—how will he not also, along with him, graciously give us all things?"

"There is . . . a time to be silent and a time to speak." Now that God has spoken to us in his Word, let us bow our heads and speak to him in prayer.

Heavenly Father, we treasure our conversations with you. Continue to speak to us in your Word. Hear and answer our prayers for Jesus' sake. Amen.

Then we cried out to the LORD, the God of our Fathers, and the LORD heard our voice and saw our misery, toil and oppression. (Deuteronomy 26:7)

GOD HEARS AND SEES HIS PEOPLE

It must have seemed to the people of Israel that God had forsaken them. Year after year their misery continued. The forced, hard labor never lightened. The number of Hebrew baby boys dumped into the Nile River grew by the month. During that long period, "The Israelites groaned in their slavery and cried out, and their cry for help because of their slavery went up to God" (Exodus 2:23).

The people must have thought, "Doesn't God hear us? Doesn't he see what we are suffering?" Unknown to them, God was already at work to answer their prayers. Moses tells us, "God heard their groaning and he remembered his covenant with Abraham, with Isaac and with Jacob. So God looked on the Israelites and was concerned about them."

Note what moved God to answer their prayer. It was not that they were such good people. Rather it was God's own promise made to their fathers Abraham, Isaac and Jacob. To abandon Israel to misery and oppression in Egypt would be breaking his own promise. This God could not do, and so he planned Israel's deliverance.

God's answer to Israel's prayers did not come immediately. God saved Moses from death in the Nile and had him trained in the Pharaoh's palace for forty years. When Moses killed the Egyptian slavemaster, he chose the wrong time and the wrong way to deliver Israel. He had to flee and live in Midian. Finally when Moses was eighty, God brought him back to Egypt to deliver Israel.

When we cry to God for help in time of need or misery, he does not always answer our prayer right away. But God sees and hears us just as surely as he did Israel and for the same reason. Not because we are such good people who deserve to have our prayers answered, but because he has made us his people by the death of his Son for us. Not to answer our prayers would be a denial of his own promise to be with us and help us.

Like Moses we must learn not to try to force the how or the when. All we need to know is that he sees and hears. Therefore, we are also sure that he is working out his answer for us in the way and at the time which his wisdom knows is best.

Lord, because you love me in your Son, I know that you see my troubles and hear my prayers. Help me patiently await your answers in the way and at the time your mercy chooses. Amen.

"In those days and at that time I will make a righteous Branch sprout from David's line." (Jeremiah 33:15)

IN GOD'S OWN TIME

Perhaps some of us remember the name Rudy Vallee. He was an extremely popular crooner in the days of megaphones and raccoon coats. One of his hit songs was entitled "My Time Is Your Time."

The song and the singer may no longer be popular, but the idea that "my time is your time" certainly is — especially when it comes to God's fulfilling his promises to us or answering our prayers. So often people think that their time must be God's time, so that when they want something done, God had better comply with their time schedule.

But our time is not necessarily God's time. For example, God says in our text, "In those days and at that time I will make a righteous Branch sprout from David's line." No doubt Adam and Eve looked for the promised "seed of the woman" soon after God talked with them in the garden of Eden after their fall into sin. Abraham, Isaac, Jacob and all of the children of Israel looked for and longed for the fulfillment of that promise. But the Savior did not come until that time and those days when God in his infinite wisdom felt it was right. And that several thousand years after Adam and Eve or the patriarchs.

Unlike sinful, limited human beings God sees the history of the world as well as the history of our lives in one panoramic view. With wisdom that often goes beyond our understanding, he maps and measures things out so that his eternal will may be done. He does things in his own good time and in his own wise way. His time and his way often may not coincide with our desires or expectations at all.

We need to remember that when it comes to God's promise to hear and answer our prayers. We may pray for something like the recovery from an illness or a special blessing from God or a change in our life, and expect the answer immediately. God promises that he will hear and answer every prayer brought to him in Jesus' name. But when and how he answers them, we must leave up to his infinite wisdom. Concerning the coming of the promised Savior Galatians 4:4 states: "But when the fulness of the time was come, God sent forth his Son" (KJV). So when the time is right in God's eyes, he will answer our prayers and fulfill his promises. Let us with patience and complete trust in the wisdom of our God bring our prayers before his throne. We know that God declares, "My time is not your time."

Dear heavenly Father, help us to understand that your time is not our time, and give us patience to await your answer to our prayers. Amen.

How long, O LORD, must I call for help, but you do not listen? Or cry out to you, "Violence!" but you do not save? (Habakkuk 1:2)

HELP US IN OUR DAY OF TROUBLE

Many of us feel it and have said it, "God does not answer my prayers." The day of trouble comes upon us, and we pray. We ask God to remove our trouble and give us happy days. We become frustrated because our trouble remains, and we seem to face only gloom. Is it true that God does not hear me? Is it true that he helps others but has no concern for me?

Habakkuk and other believers in his day felt this way. The powerful and wealthy abused the weak and poor. Life was unfair and difficult for the majority of the people. Why did not God help when the believers called upon him in prayer? Didn't he see, hear or care?

Is there an answer to such questions? There most surely is. Through faith in Jesus Christ we are God's forgiven and saved children. Our Father hears our prayers. However, he does not comply with our wishes or commands as to how and when our prayers are to be answered. Rather we are to acknowledge his wisdom, trust his love, and submit to his good and gracious will. The Apostle John tells us, "This is the confidence we have in approaching God: that if we ask anything according to his will, he hears us." He has promised to give us strength for carrying our burdens and to make all things work together for our good. He will remove our troubles if and when it is best for us.

God is not lying when he commands and promises, "Call upon me in the day of trouble: I will deliver you, and you will honor me." If we pray to the true God with confidence, he hears and answers every prayer. He gave his only Son to suffer and die and earn our salvation. He will also help us with our lesser needs.

Christians daily pray to God in the name of our Lord Jesus Christ. He wants us to pray to him as we face this life's frustrations. He hears the prayers of his believers. He will help us in frustration, trouble and terror.

Father, help us in our day of trouble. Answer our prayers in your best way and at your best time. We ask this in Jesus' name. Amen.

In my distress I called to the LORD; I cried to my God for help. From his temple he heard my voice; my cry came before him, into his ears. (Psalm 18:6)

PRAYER IN A TRAGIC HOUR

This beautiful psalm directs our hearts to prayer in time of tragedy. In the extremity of Jesus' suffering his nation had rejected him, his Father in heaven had forsaken him, and yet he cried out, "Father, into your hands I commit my spirit." The Father in heaven heard the prayer of his beloved Son and sustained him in the awesome task of saving the world. In his tragic hour Christ prayed.

The Bible is filled with examples of prayer. All of the great people of faith prayed. They prayed in time of distress as well as at other times. "Prayer is the Christian's vital breath."

Our tragic hours are nothing when compared to those which Christ spent as he bore the weight of the sins of the world. Nonetheless, our trials and afflictions represent difficulties for us. Particularly does Satan like to whisper to us amidst our troubles, "See, God doesn't really love you after all. Doesn't this problem prove it?" If ever anyone could have felt forsaken of God, it was Christ. But what did he do? He prayed.

Is some besetting sin getting you down? Is some illness continuing without relief? Is sorrow filling your heart at the loss of a loved one? Take it to the Lord in prayer. He commanded us to pray and has promised to hear us. And having taken it to the Lord in prayer, you will learn to say with Job of old, "Though he slay me, yet will I hope in him." With the psalmist we will say, "The LORD is near to all who call on him, to all who call on him in truth. He fulfills the desires of those who fear him; he hears their cry and saves them."

Surely in these latter days of sore distress we all have reason enough to fall upon our knees before our God. Let us pray boldly and confidently knowing that "The prayer of a righteous man is powerful and effective." It is God's desire to bless us and he himself has bid us to pray. "Let us then approach the throne of grace with confidence, so that we may receive mercy and find grace to help us in our time of need."

Lord, show me what I have to do;
Every hour my strength renew.
Let me live a life of faith;
Let me die Thy people's death. Amen.

53

Yet you brought me out of the womb; you made me trust in you even at my mother's breast. From birth I was cast upon you; from my mother's womb you have been my God. Do not be far from me, for trouble is near and there is no one to help. (Psalm 22:9-11)

NOT MY WILL, BUT YOURS BE DONE

One of the most difficult prayers to pray is the one which Jesus uttered in Gethsemane: "Not my will, but yours be done." When we have some plan or hope which is very dear to us, it is extremely difficult for us to give it up. We may even feel resentful or bitter that God doesn't see the matter our way.

Jesus, the Lamb of God, had prayed: "My Father, if it is possible, may this cup be taken from me." The prospect of the agony and the pain he would have to endure was almost unendurable. But it could not be any other way! Paying for the sins of the world demanded the sacrifice of the Lamb of God.

Thank God, that in the midst of this desperate situation the Savior still clung to God in faith. As he considered his earthly life, he realized that he had a special position in God's plans for men. From his birth on God had already marked him for special service. That God had led him to the cross had changed nothing. That, too, was part of the eternal plan to save sinners. Thus he trusted that, in spite of being forsaken, he was still an object of great concern to his Father. Even though rebuffed by God, he still sought to remain close to God and recognized him as his only Helper. When he gave up the spirit, it was with the confidence that God was still backing him. For he said, "Father, into your hands I commit my spirit."

Jesus was sure that God's will was a good and gracious will. We have the same conviction as we ponder the death of Christ. Although no life, no work, could have come to a more ignominious or disastrous end than that of our Savior, yet we know that it was not a disaster. That's why we sing: "In the cross of Christ I glory." Christ was faithful to the end. In this Christ was not only our Savior but also our model.

When the answer to our prayers is different than we expect, when the goal we pursue escapes our grasp, it's not really the end of the world. We have the confidence that God has something in mind for us which is wiser and more beneficial—if we too are faithful to the end, as the Savior was.

What God ordains is always good; His will abideth holy.
As He directs my life for me, I follow meek and lowly.
My God indeed in every need Doth well know how to shield me;
To Him, then, I will yield me. Amen.

Turn your ear to me, come quickly to my rescue; be my rock of refuge, a strong fortress to save me.(Psalm 31:2)

HEAR ME AND HASTEN TO HELP

Bow down Thy gracious ear to me
And hear my cries and prayers to Thee,
Haste Thee for my protection;
For woes and fear Surround me here.
Help me in mine affliction.

(TLH 524:2)

The vitality of the Bible is indestructible. No condition or circumstance of human life ever comes but the Bible has a word to meet it exactly. Every word of the Thirty-First Psalm shows us that troubles do come to the children of God. God's people are not exempt from blighting burdens, searing sorrows, perplexing problems, and distressing discouragements. Afflictions and adversities, temptations and trials, bitter experiences and painful sufferings are the lot of God's children.

These things are not due, as some say, to sin on the Christian's part. When you turn to the Word of God, it is perfectly clear on this point. There you hear God say: "The Lord disciplines those he loves." "In this world," says Jesus, "you will have trouble." This is one of the most expressive words in the Bible. But he goes on to add the all-conquering promise: "But take heart! I have overcome the world."

Yes, troubles do come. But we need not give way to despair. We have God and his Word on which we can lean, in which we can trust for help and deliverance. There is a German proverb which says: "Need teaches us to pray." And pray we can, and shall, as David did: "Turn your ear to me"—give attention to my prayer, for you promised: "He will call upon me, and I will answer him; I will be with him in trouble, I will deliver him and honor him." Yes, God knows, God hears, God answers every prayer of a believing child of his.

"Come quickly to my rescue." David's need was great and urgent. Enemies were all about him, threatening to crush him. So it sometimes is with us. The unholy three—the devil, the world and the flesh—are always at us with temptations, trials, hatred, ridicule, persecution. And this is not all; there are afflictions that help to make up the cross laid upon us. But we need not fear. We have God's promise: "Call upon me in the day of trouble; I will deliver you, and you will honor me." So we pray:

In God, my faithful God,
I trust when dark my road;
Tho' many woes o'ertake me,
Yet He will not forsake me.
His love it is doth send them
And, when 'tis best, will end them

"So be it," then I say
With all my heart each day.
We, too, dear Lord, adore Thee,
We sing for joy before Thee.
Guide us while here we wander
Until we praise Thee yonder. Amen.

Cast your cares (burden-KJV) on the LORD and he will sustain you; he will never let the righteous fall. (Psalm 55:22)

INVITATION TO PRAYER

"Burden" is a heavy word, one of those words which sounds like its meaning. The weight of the problem can be felt even as the word is spoken. As we consider what we ought to do in the hour of need, we hear the advice of the psalmist that we are to seek the help of the Lord.

Seeking help is a regular part of our lives. As differing needs arise, we seek help from those who are able to grant it. The medical doctor cares for our physical ailments, the lawyer unwinds our legal entanglements, the mechanic solves our automotive dilemmas, and so forth. Only the foolish seek no help from the proper source when it is readily available. Only the foolish would seek help for their bodies from a mechanic or for their car from a doctor. Help from the wrong source is no help at all.

As we Christians go through life, there is one common source of help for us in any problem, one individual who can be approached whatever our need. That special source of help is our God. He can and will guide us in every undertaking, as he has promised.

But there is another side to God's invitation. If we do not bring our problems to him in faith, if we continue to worry or fret in the face of problems in spite of his invitation, then we are actually showing a lack of confidence in him and his promise. Even the best Christian is guilty of this weakness from time to time. We have to remember that God didn't say "sometimes" he would help, "sometimes" he would be available, or that he is available only for large burdens. Every problem, every care should be brought to him for help. Not to do so is a vote of "no confidence" in his offer.

In this 55th Psalm, as in so many of them, the psalmist speaks of his enemy. As we pray these same psalms, we understand that enemy to be Satan and the temptations and trials that he sets before us. In the face of all such, we are told simply to "cast your cares on the Lord." All of Scripture is filled with the message of God's love for sinners, his gift of forgiveness and eternal life, his offer to guide and protect each of us on the road to our eternal joy. How simple it is to relax with our cares given over to God, to sing his praises without hindrance from worry or care.

Almighty God, help me to see the joy of giving all my burden of care over to you at your invitation. Amen.

He will call upon me, and I will answer him; I will be with him in trouble, I will deliver him and honor him. (Psalm 91:15)

GOD'S PROMISE TO ANSWER PRAYER

You and I live in a world of change. Governments rise and fall; cities grow and then crumble into dust, clothes you wore just last year are relegated to the rag bag before they are worn out, simply because they are out of style. We see it also in the people around us. We are born, we live and grow, and then we die. Truly, as the hymn writer says: "Change and decay in all around I see."

In view of this it is a comfort to the Christian to know that there are still some things that do not change and never will. In the book of the Prophet Malachi God says, "I am the Lord, I change not." Yes, God never changes. And because God never changes, his Word never changes. It is still the same for all people everywhere. Our salvation in Jesus Christ is firm and sure. Also, because God never changes, his promises never do. When God makes a promise, we can be absolutely sure that he will keep it. There is nothing more certain than that.

Just think of how God has kept his promises to the saints down through history. God made this promise: "He will call upon Me, and I will answer him." So God-fearing Hannah prayed for children, and a son was born. Elijah called out to God before the prophets of Baal on Mt. Carmel, and heaven rained fire to receive the sacrifice. Hezekiah called on the Lord, and the power of Syria died in the night. Elisha reached out to the Lord of Hosts, and chariots and horsemen of fire filled the mountain. Daniel turned to the Lord in prayer, and the angel closed the mouths of the lions. The church at Jerusalem prayed, and St. Peter marched out of prison.

Perhaps there is some trouble that lies heavy on our heart this very day. Do we need some spiritual gift? Is it the Holy Spirit? Is it an increase of faith or of knowledge? Is it the assurance of pardon, peace or eternal salvation? Whatever it is, let us cast our burden upon the Lord. Let us remember the unchanging promise that God has made to us: "He will call upon me, and I will answer him: I will be with him in trouble." That is a promise God made to us. We can be sure that it will never change.

Lord, place into my hands this sword of assurance and strength that you will always keep your word. Amen.

Who forgives all your sins and heals all your diseases, who redeems your life from the pit and crowns you with love and compassion, who satisfies your desires with good things so that your youth is renewed like the eagle's. (Psalm 103:3-5)

PRAY WITH THANKFUL HEARTS

Have you seen choir singers who looked sad when they sang the most joyful music? Pity the director! He hears grumbling about rehearsals. He knows the jealousy one singer might have toward another. He may even have contributed to his choir's bad attitude by recruiting singers with no better inducements than "We need your strong voice," or "We're short an alto."

In our text, David is recruiting a choir. But see how he does it! There must be no reluctance in this choir, no halfhearted singing. The "singers" are to be all the parts of himself—his soul, heart, body, strength, mouth. To his "singers" David says, "Now let us bless the Lord, all that is within me!"

Why this singing? First of all, David says to himself, "Because the Lord heals all your diseases."

When a broken arm knits together, it's because God gives human bones the ability to mend themselves. When surgeon and medicine combine to relieve suffering, it's because God willed it. That's why Christians bless him.

He has redeemed my life from destruction. Many times, often without my knowing it, God has spared me from accidents and injury. But the deepest pit from which he pulled me up is the fiery abyss of hell. It cost him something—his own Son and his Son's blood. Therefore, choir-within-myself, bless his name!

God has "crowned" me with love and compassion. He wants me to know that I wear, like a richly jeweled crown upon my head, all the daily blessings that flow out of His devoted heart. Wearing my gift-crown, I bow before the Giver's throne and praise his name.

Daily God gives me what my body needs. Not spoiled food, poison or the "defiled bread" of Ezekiel's day, but good things does God place into my mouth. An eagle symbolizes strength. A golden eagle has the strength to carry a fawn or collie to its nest. All its life the eagle appears young and powerful. So God renews me, refreshing me both spiritually and bodily.

Gladly I salute such goodness. Choir-of-all-my-being, joyfully sing to God's gracious name!

I bless you for your loving-kindness towards me, O Triune God, especially for redeeming me through the precious blood of Christ. Amen.

My God, my God, why have you forsaken me? Why are you so far from saving me, so far from the words of my groaning? O my God, I cry out by day, but you do not answer, by night, and am not silent. Yet you are enthroned as the Holy One; you are the praise of Israel. In you our fathers put their trust; they trusted and you delivered them. They cried to you and were saved; in you they trusted and were not disappointed. But I am a worm and not a man, scorned by men and despised by the people. (Psalm 22:1-6)

ACCEPTED BECAUSE HE WAS REJECTED

How comforting it is for us in a time of grief or trouble to be able to turn to our gracious Lord in prayer! How reassuring it is for us, when everything seems to go wrong, to know what a Friend we have in Jesus! This has been the experience of the people of God of all times. Even before David's time the "fathers" trusted in God, and they were delivered. They were not confounded.

But what a different situation confronted the Lamb of God, Jesus Christ! He is treated like a worm. Men despise him and reproach him. They treat him as less than human. How arrogantly his enemies strut up and down before his cross and cruelly mock him! Friend and foe alike are a source of agony and suffering to him.

So he applies the time-tested solution of turning to God. But even this avenue is closed to him. God has forsaken him too. He asks plaintively why this should be, but in his heart of hearts he knows. It is because he is "the Lamb of God, who takes away the sin of the world." As the Lamb of God, he must die. He must become a Substitute for all sinners. He must die the death we should have died. He must be separated from God and forsaken by him, although it is we who should have been. This is the depth of his love, that he was willing to endure this for our sake!

Because he was forsaken by God, we need not fear that God will forsake us. Because he was refused by the heavenly Father in his search for help, we are accepted by this same Father. Now our prayers in the name of the Lamb of God find ready acceptance and a proper answer.

O Christ, Lamb of God, you have taken away the sin of the world; have mercy on us and grant us your peace. Many times we have felt driven into a corner, but none of our problems can ever equal yours. Let your great love for us increase our love for you. Fill us with a measure of the courage and strength with which you suffered such great rejection that we may not lose heart, nor murmur, nor complain. Make us patient and enduring for your name's sake. Amen.

See, I have refined you, though not as silver; I have tested you in the furnace of affliction. (Isaiah 48:10)

IN GRACE GOD SHAPES OUR LIVES

How would we describe our daily living? Would we be able to say that we are the masters of our own lives and destinies? We would like to be able to plot out for ourselves our entire life. In it we would place the things that we feel would be good for us. A student may decide to enter a certain type of school to prepare for a profession or trade. A young couple may put off marriage to a later date in order to be free to do what they want without being encumbered by family obligations. A husband and wife may want to build up for themselves a little nest egg so that they will be able to purchase the things they deem necessary.

Note that, in all such planning, little thought may be given to the fact that we really are not the masters of our destiny. There is One who rules our lives. And we soon see how little we are able to carry out everything that we had planned for ourselves.

We may have thought we were planning for our benefit, but God saw it to be otherwise. God had his own plans. When we wanted to do one thing with our life, God did something else. God has refined us in the furnace of affliction, which burns but does not destroy.

It is a marvel to watch workmen start just with the raw material and from that progress slowly and patiently to fashion an object of beauty. In their own way they subject the material they work with to certain stresses and strains. It may appear as if they were destroying the material. However, in the end they have made an object of great value.

So the Lord makes and fashions us into something of great value: from that which is tainted with sin and apart from the Lord, to that which has been set aside for the glory and honor of God. He cleanses us by the blood of Jesus Christ, his Son. With the Gospel he calls us to faith in the Savior, Jesus. God continues to refine us, sanctifying and keeping us in the true faith for time and for eternity. God allows certain crosses and trials to enter our lives in order to strengthen our faith and to keep us as his special people.

Lord of grace, refine our faith and keep us in your love as your people. Amen.

Why have you made me your target? Have I become a burden to you? Why do you not pardon my offenses and forgive my sins? (Job 7:20,21)

WHY ME?

Why? That is the question that comes immediately to the minds of even the most faithful in times of great suffering or tribulation. "Why me?" asks the man stricken with cancer, or the wife who has just lost her husband and has to bring up four children alone. Even the strongest Christians are likely to lift their eyes to heaven and ask, "Why, Lord?" if they lose their home in a tornado or by fire.

Even Job, whose patience is proverbial, had to carry his plaintive query to the throne of heaven itself. He was trying to comprehend the mysterious workings of God as he deals with his saints on earth. Why Lord, why? Maybe I'm wrong; maybe I'm not forgiven. Why don't you pardon my transgression and take away mine iniquity?

Job knew the promise of forgiveness through the Redeemer who would come. But he just didn't feel forgiven. He couldn't comprehend why a gracious and loving God would afflict the very person who believed in him and who constantly tried to do his will.

Job was finally forced to these conclusions: either he was no child of God, and he knew that wasn't true; or God must act arbitrarily without regard to the state of the person whom he afflicts, and that answer didn't satisfy either. Thus, throughout the book, Job continued to ask why. He constantly wished that the Almighty himself would explain to him the reason behind such unbearable suffering.

When problems of suffering wear us down, we, too, often demand to look into the innermost recesses of the mind of God. We also want everything to be explained to us. We cry out "Why?" and sometimes feel that God must be punishing us.

Like Job, we have to learn to bear with patience our afflictions and not doubt that "in all things God works for the good of those who love him." We need to see that it is the love of a Father that chastens us and purifies our love for him. We need to see that nothing can separate us from the love of God, which is in Christ Jesus our Lord.

Job never received a direct answer to all his questions, but he was led to see that the Lord is gracious after all. We, too, will someday see the purpose of all God does with us, if not here, certainly in heaven. Let us trust him, then, rather than speculate about why.

Lord, give me a heart that accepts all things with patience. Amen.

Then the Lord said to Satan, "Have you considered my servant Job? There is no one on earth like him; he is blameless and upright, a man who fears God and shuns evil. And he still maintains his integrity, though you incited me against him to ruin him without any reason." (Job 2:3)

TRIALS—PUNISHMENT OR OPPORTUNITY?

"Who sinned, this man or his parents, that he was born blind?" the disciples asked Jesus one day. They were under the common impression that when misfortune strikes, when everything goes wrong, when there is extreme suffering, it must be a punishment for some great sin. Jesus set them straight. The man was not blind as a result of anyone's special sin, "but this happened so that the work of God might be displayed in his life" (John 9:3).

Job had lost everything. And worse was yet to come. He would lose even his health. In the midst of his suffering, though, all that his friends could think of to comfort him was to tell him that his suffering must be a punishment for some great hidden sin. If he would only repent, everything would be all right again.

The only problem with this advice was that Job had been repentant all along. His faith had been in his Redeemer from the very beginning. He knew it and for that reason rejected his friends' counsel. God knew it too. That's why, in the middle of Job's misfortune, he called Job, "my servant," and "blameless and upright, a man who fears God and shuns evil." Even though Job had lost everything, "he still maintains his integrity." Job's suffering wasn't a punishment. It was an opportunity for this man of faith to hold to his Lord in bad times as well as in good.

When trouble strikes, a job is lost, sickness incapacitates, or a loved one dies, it is good to know that we are still the servants of God through faith in Christ. God himself will say so, just as he praised Job.

As Christians we believe, "there is now no condemnation for those who are in Christ Jesus" (Romans 8:1). There are tests. There are helpful chastisements. But our punishment has already been borne by our Savior, Jesus Christ.

Heroic faith in times of adversity is a faith like Job's. It trusts that God is still with us, still loves us and still calls us his servants.

Lord, give me a strong faith when the dark clouds of adversity threaten, so that I may be comforted by the promise of your everlasting love in Christ Jesus. Amen.

He replied, "I have been very zealous for the Lord God Almighty. The Israelites have rejected your covenant, broken down your altars, and put your prophets to death with the sword. I am the only one left, and now they are trying to kill me too." (1 Kings 19:14)

"IT'S ME AGAINST THE WORLD, GOD"

"It's me against the world, God." Do you recognize this as the almost helpless cry of the beleaguered Christian? It certainly was the cry of the prophet Elijah after his struggle with the prophets of Baal. Just put yourself in his position. He had showed the prophets of Baal on Mt. Carmel who the true God was. .them in the Kishon Valley. What thanks did he get? The king's wife, Jezebel, gave orders for Elijah to be killed.

Elijah, mighty man of God, became the prophet the government sought to silence permanently. Instead of waiting around to be caught and killed, Elijah quickly fled for his life. After running for awhile, he decided it was time to have a talk with God. "I have had enough, Lord. Take my life." In other words, "That's it God. I'm through. Let someone else take the hassle."

What Elijah forgot was that he was not the one who had shown the prophets of Baal who the true God was. He was not the one who made it possible for the prophets of Baal to be put to death. He did not travel for forty days and nights on his own strength. It was the Lord God Almighty who caused these things to happen.

The same Lord God Almighty sends trials into our lives. He does so to strengthen our faith. He does so to remind us that we can and should be absolutely positive that he will take good care of us. He does so to teach us to place his will above ours. He does so that we might listen and obey his word.

In our world which is so dominated by man-centered thought, "It's me against the world, God!" may become a more frequently heard cry among Christians. More and more emphasis is being placed on the indomitable spirit of man rather than on the providence of our gracious God. Many would have us believe that we can control our own destinies. Where will this all end? Let us commit our lives to the good and gracious will of the true God who answers our prayers and rescues us from every evil.

Lord, keep us steadfast in Thy Word;
Curb those who fain by craft and sword
Would wrest the Kingdom from Thy Son
And set at naught all He hath done. Amen.

The L ORD is good to those whose hope is in him, to the one who seeks him; it is good to wait quietly for the salvation of the L ORD . It is good for a man to bear the yoke while he is young. (Lamentations 3:25-27)

THE LORD DISCIPLINES THOSE HE LOVES

A knife, a saw, an axe—these are instruments designed to cut and to sever. In the wrong hands they can murder or destroy or vandalize, but in the skillful hands of a trained orchardist these same tools can be useful in producing healthy trees which produce bountiful crops. The orchardman uses these tools to cut branches and to prune diseased or excess stock. An untrained observer might be shocked at the appearance of "wanton destruction," but if it were not done, the orchard would quickly deteriorate; because it is done, the orchard flourishes.

Israel's suffering at the hands of its enemies, your suffering a severe financial setback, my grief over the loss of a loved one—these, too, are examples of painful but necessary experiences for those involved. Today's Scripture reading reminds us again that "the Lord disciplines those he loves." A person who doesn't know any better might be led to believe that those who were enduring these or similar afflictions were being punished for some grievous crime of theirs. But a child of God knows that the Lord must also "prune his trees." He must sometimes lay a yoke upon the necks of his people to chasten them because he loves them. "It is good for a man that he bear the yoke."

Our parents, in love, have corrected us; we correct our own children because we are concerned about their spiritual development. Children who are corrected will not turn against their parents, but in later years will bless and thank them every day. The writer to the Hebrews says, "The Lord disciplines those he loves, and he punishes [that is, corrects] everyone he accepts as a son. Endure hardship as discipline; God is treating you as sons. For what son is not disciplined by his father? If you are not disciplined (and everyone undergoes discipline), then you are illegitimate children and not true sons. Moreover, we have all had human fathers who disciplined us and we respected them for it. How much more should we submit to the Father of our spirits and live!" (Hebrews 12:6-9)

Let us be reminded once again that through his discipline our loving Father does whatever needs to be done so that we might be and remain his heirs, here and hereafter.

What God ordains is always good,
His loving thought attends me;
No poison can be in the cup
That my Physician sends me.
My God is true; Each morn anew
I'll trust his grace unending,
My life to Him commending. Amen.

Let him sit alone in silence, for the Lord has laid it on him. Let him bury his face in the dust—there may yet be hope. Let him offer his cheek to one who would strike him, and let him be filled with disgrace. (Lamentations 3:28-30)

WAIT IN HUMBLE SUBMISSION

In these verses we are again reminded of the severe strokes of God's chastening rod which fell upon Israel during the years of the Babylonian Captivity. And yet the believers among the people of this exiled nation were able to endure this misery in patient submission. They humbled themselves under the mighty hand of God. The fact of God's loving concern may not have been evident in the midst of all this misery, but God's people of all ages are gratefully aware that all things work together for the good of those who believe in Christ.

Sometimes, however, we may chafe and squirm under the chastenings of our loving God. We may try in vain to understand how a certain illness or sorrowful experience or tragic loss can possibly be for our well-being. The Lord does not say that we shall always be able to understand immediately and clearly why he is chastening us. It ought to be enough for those whom he loves to know that his ways are not always our ways.

Remember that "thorn in the flesh" which the Apostle Paul speaks about in Second Corinthians? He did not know either, exactly or specifically, just what God's reasons were for permitting him to suffer this affliction. But he endured in humble submission. He writes: "To keep me from becoming conceited because of these surpassingly great revelations, there was given me a thorn in my flesh, a messenger of Satan, to torment me. Three times I pleaded with the Lord to take it away from me. But he said to me, 'My grace is sufficient for you, for my power is made perfect in weakness' " (2 Corinthians 12:7-9).

So here we do have an answer to the questions a Christian may have concerning life in this vale of tears. The Lord's chastisements may have the dual purpose of keeping us from becoming proud and of fortifying our faith so that we might serve him better. With Paul we can "delight in weaknesses. . . . For when I am weak, then I am strong" (2 Corinthians 12:10) in Christ.

The will of God is always best
And shall be done forever
And they who trust in Him are blest;
He will forsake them never.
He helps indeed In time of need,
He chastens with forbearing;
They who depend On God, their Friend,
Shall not be left despairing.
May this, Lord, be our comfort. Amen.

65

And Ruth the Moabitess said to Naomi, "Let me go to the fields and pick up the leftover grain behind anyone in whose eyes I find favor." Naomi said to her, "Go ahead, my daughter." So she went out and began to glean in the fields behind the harvesters. As it turned out, she found herself working in a field belonging to Boaz, who was from the clan of Elimelech. (Ruth 2:2,3)

THINGS DON'T JUST HAPPEN

How different would your life have been if you had risen an hour later this morning? If you had taken a different route to work last week? If you had moved east instead of west? If you had married someone else instead of your present spouse? On seemingly simple and straightforward occurrences often hang the major events of our lives, and sometimes even the difference between life and death itself.

Take Ruth, for example. She and her mother-in-law, Naomi, had no means of support, so she volunteered to go and pick up cuttings of grain left behind after the reapers went through a field. We are told simply, "it turned out, she found herself working in a field belonging to Boaz." Ruth just "happened" to pick the field of Boaz.

Boaz was a close relative of Ruth's late husband and therefore, according to Levitical law, in line to assume the care of the dead man's property and wife. And thus it turned out that in time Boaz and Ruth were married. Ruth had found herself a kind and loving husband. Boaz had acquired a wife as beautiful of heart as of appearance. And a child was born to them that would be the ancestor of Jesus the Messiah. All because Ruth "happened" to choose that one particular field to work that day.

Of course, we would be missing the point if we believed these events just "happened." The Lord with his gracious hand was guiding the lives of these people. He was seeing to it that events occurred in such a way to accomplish his good purpose.

In this way he guides also our lives. He allows things to happen which to us may seem indeed to be blessings, or may appear to be punishments, or, most frequently, are unnoticed altogether. Yet, these "happenings" are the workings of our Father, performed in our best interests. He invested the life of his only Son in our eternal welfare. Certainly he is also taking care of us in this life.

Therefore we shall not want to exclude him from anything in our lives. We shall be anxious to consult him before every decision and every undertaking, no matter how insignificant it might seem. And we shall accept his guidance and thank him for it.

I thank you, dear Lord, for your hand in my life. Amen.

Then Joseph said to his brothers, "Come close to me." When they had done so, he said, "I am your brother Joseph, the one you sold into Egypt! And now, do not be distressed and do not be angry with yourselves for selling me here, because it was to save lives that God sent me ahead of you. For two years now there has been famine in the land, and for the next five years there will not be plowing and reaping. But God sent me ahead of you to preserve for you a remnant on earth and to save your lives by a great deliverance. So then, it was not you who sent me here, but God. He made me father to Pharaoh, lord of his entire household and ruler of all Egypt." (Genesis 45:4-8)

ALL THINGS WORK TOGETHER FOR GOOD

"We'll fix him!" With that, Joseph's jealous brothers sold him into slavery in Egypt. Their evil deed removed him from their sight. Not even the unexpected depths of their father's grief could bring them to admit that they had acted rashly and sinfully.

God knew what they were planning, saw what they did and used even this horrible sin against Joseph and their father Jacob to bring about a means to save them ten years later. It is hard for us to understand, how God uses even the evil deeds of evil men to work good for his own. Our question always seems to be, "Why did God permit such a thing to happen?" It is a rather foolish question when we consider that we cannot understand God's ways while we live in a world of sin. The "face to face" seeing (1 Corinthians 13:12) won't be ours until God brings us to heaven.

The best solution for the Christian who is having difficulty understanding what is going on around him is to follow the example of Joseph, who kept his faith focused on his heavenly Father. When he faces his brothers later in Egypt, he realizes the guiding hand of God, which used the evil intended by his brothers for the good of all of them.

Though we may from time to time be able to see, as Joseph did, how God's plan for us unfolds, more often we must simply step forward in faith, knowing God's wisdom and might have the situation well in hand. We can say with David, "My eyes are ever on the LORD" (Psalm 25:15). We read with joy the words which God caused Paul to set forth so clearly, "We know that in all things God works for the good of those who love him" (Romans 8:28). God has clearly told us so!

My God hath all things in His keeping,
He is the ever faithful Friend;
He grants me laughter after weeping,
And all His ways in blessing end.
His love endures eternally;
What pleaseth God, that pleaseth me. Amen.

(Jacob) My father was a wandering Aramean, and he went down to Egypt with a few people and lived there and became a great nation, powerful and numerous. (Deuteronomy 26:5)

A DETOUR FOR A PURPOSE

One of God's precious promises which meant a great deal to the Old Testament Christian was that God would give his people their own land. This would make the event spoken about in our text somewhat surprising. Jacob and his family were living in that promised land, but God uprooted them and sent them down to Egypt. This was only a detour, not a loss of the promised land. And it was a detour for a purpose.

That purpose is hinted at by the words, "He went down into Egypt with a few people . . . and became a great nation, powerful, and numerous." When Jacob and his family went down to Egypt, they numbered seventy. When Israel left Egypt under Moses, they numbered a million, perhaps two million. God took his people to Egypt that they might develop into a large and powerful nation.

But couldn't they have developed into such a nation while living in the promised land? Yes, they could have. But by the time this would have come about, Israel most likely would have been a nation as corrupt as the Canaanites who lived in that same land. Genesis 34 and 38 tell us how easily Jacob's sons were led into moral misconduct by the people living around them.

How was Egypt different? Joseph told his father Jacob that, when he moved with his family to Egypt, they would be put in Goshen because "all shepherds are detestable to the Egyptians." The grain farmers of Egypt would have nothing to do with these shepherds. So the Israelites could live in isolation until they would develop into "a great nation, powerful and numerous."

Detours for a purpose. God also takes us on them in our lives. When we think we are settled into a life which is best for us, unexpectedly God takes us on a detour. Why? For our spiritual good. It was not best for Jacob's family to remain in Palestine. We can be just as sure, if God takes our life on a detour, he is doing it according to his plan of what is best for us. We are his people whom he bought for himself by Jesus' blood. He is leading us on the way to our eternal promised land in heaven. Every detour on which our loving Maker and Savior takes us is intended to bring us safely to that goal.

Lord, lead us to accept the detours in our life as part of the map you have laid out to bring us to yourself in heaven. Amen.

But God remembered Noah and all the wild animals and the livestock that were with him in the ark. (Genesis 8:1)

WAITING FOR DELIVERANCE

We sit in our snug homes and after two or three days of cloudy, rainy weather sadly ask, "Is this rain ever going to quit?" Think of Noah and his family. They had to endure 40 days and nights of a torrential downpour from the heavens and a gushing upheaval out of the earth.

Then followed month after month of waiting within the ark while the waters still covered the earth. How often they must have been tempted to doubt for their safety, asking first if the ark would be able to stand the heavy downpour, then if it would float, and then if it could keep from foundering or capsizing as the waters carried it here and there.

As the days gave way to weeks, and the weeks to months, the hardest trial of all must have been to keep their patience. They must often have asked, "Has God forgotten us? Is there no end to the flood? Shall we never leave this ark?"

Scripture says, "And God remembered Noah." Did he ever forget him? Of course not. Could he ever have forgotten him? Of course not. The only thing that God can and

does forget regarding his people is their sin. "For I will forgive their wickedness and will remember their sins no more" (Jeremiah 31:34). But his people he cannot forget. "Can a mother forget the baby at her breast and have no compassion on the child she has borne? Though she may forget, I will not forget you!" (Isaiah 49:15)

"God remembered Noah" means that God, mindful of his promise, mercifully delivered Noah at the right time and in the right way. God so ordered things. The waters went down. The day finally came when Noah and his family could step out on dry ground once more.

Waiting for deliverance is often hard for a Christian. When the days and nights are long, it is easy for the Christian to think that God has forgotten. We should learn from Noah to send such thoughts right back where they come from, namely, the devil who tempts us to sin.

"God remembered Noah." And he also remembers us in his goodness and mercy. Therefore he must and will deliver us, though for the moment he may appear to have hidden his face from us.

Blessed Savior, strengthen us by your Spirit, that in our trials we may never despair of your gracious mercy, help and deliverance. Amen.

I have set the LORD always before me. Because he is at my right hand, I will not be shaken. (Psalm 16:8)

REMEMBER AND APPLY GOD'S WORD

We know that God is our trusted advisor, who provides us with guidance for every day of our lives. But no matter how good an advisor is, he cannot help anyone who does not remember his advice or put it into practice. The guidance we receive from God's Word will benefit us only if we remember it and apply it.

In our text David says, "I have set the LORD always before me." When David went to face Goliath, he took the Lord with him. When he was driven from his home and from the Lord's tabernacle, first by Saul, then by his son Absalom, he took the Lord with him. He could do this because he kept God's Word in his heart. He remembered the things he had learned from his childhood. In some of the darkest hours of his life he wrote some of his most beautiful psalms.

David not only remembered God's Word, he also applied it at the critical times when his faith was tested. When David had the opportunity to kill Saul, he did not do it. He trusted the Lord to deliver him in his own good time. In some of the most terrible trials David kept the Lord always before him. This was not a foolish dream or wishful thinking on David's part. The Lord was not present only in David's mind. He really was at David's right hand, saving him from death time after time. Even when David forgot God and fell into sin, the Lord returned to him and called him to repentance through the prophet Nathan. Even through their best calculated efforts Saul and Absalom could not destroy David. Even with his most diabolical temptations Satan could not tear David away from the Lord. Because the Lord is strong and unshakable, David could not be shaken. David felt secure because he remembered God, but David was secure, in fact, because God remembered him. God remembered his promises to David, and he fulfilled them, not only when David was faithful, but even when David stumbled and fell.

We have promises as sure as those given to David. God has promised us forgiveness of sins. He has promised us eternal life. He has promised to keep us safe from every evil. Because God is unshakable, because his promises are sure, we will not be shaken. Nothing can separate us from the love of God.

Faithful Lord God, we know that we cannot find safety or peace of mind through our own efforts, but since you are at our right hand, we are confident that we will never be shaken. Amen.

The LORD said, ". . . So I have come down to rescue them from the hand of the Egyptians." (Exodus 3:8)

WORDS OF RESCUE

Remember this experience as a child. You climbed up a stepladder. Near the top you looked around and down. You saw the concrete floor was a long distance away. You tried to step down but were afraid of missing a step and falling. The icy fist of fear hit the pit of your stomach. You cried out for help. Dad heard and saw your precarious predicament. "I'll be right there to help you down," he said. What a relief those words brought. They were spoken to assure you of rescue.

Being caught on a high stepladder is a minor danger. What about being stranded on a sinking ship? Or being left in a blazing building? Or being trapped in a gas-filled mine? Should the announcement come, "We will be right there to rescue you," those words would produce a feeling of great relief.

The Lord announced to Moses, "I have come down to rescue them [the Israelites] from the hand of the Egyptians." The toil of working without rest, the whippings of the cruel master, the brutal killing of the infant sons of Israel will end. The eternal Lord was telling Moses that he could count on the rescue taking place as if it already had occurred. What relief the people of Israel must have felt when Moses repeated this divine promise to them. The danger of their own death and their nations' annihilation had been lifted.

A danger stares us in the face today. It is a danger far more serious than death through a catastrophe or extermination by a cruel government. Forever in hell is the peril. Our sin is the cause. "The wages of sin is death."

The eternal Lord spoke and announced our rescue. He proclaimed, "Christ Jesus, . . . has destroyed death." How did he accomplish this feat? "The blood of Jesus, his Son, purifies us from all sin." When did this rescue become our own? "For God so loved the world that he gave his one and only Son, that WHOEVER BELIEVES IN HIM shall not perish but have eternal life."

What a relief to hear these words! They surpass any other rescue announcement we have heard or could hear.

Eternal Lord, thank you for rescuing me from the dangerous result of sin and for announcing the good news to me through the written Word. Make me believe in this deliverance always. Amen.

Taste and see that the LORD is good; blessed is the man who takes refuge in him. (Psalm 34:8)

NOURISHED BY THE WORD

In the familiar parable of the Prodigal Son, we are told that after his "binge" of sinful self-indulgence, "there was a severe famine in that whole country, and he began to be in need." A bit later, after he had gained a lowly, filthy job feeding swine, the prodigal son lamented: "I am starving to death!" Actually that young man had unknowingly been suffering from spiritual want and hunger from the time he left his father's house. Even as he was wasting his inheritance with riotous living, stuffing himself with food and drink, and immersing himself in all sorts of sensual pleasures, that young man was a famine victim. For he failed to feed on the spiritual nourishment offered in God's Word.

So today, in the midst of a prosperous country where churches and Bibles abound, where freedom of religion is casually taken for granted, many people are hungry and in want, spiritually speaking, and worst of all, they generally do not recognize their pitiful condition. In a society that is becoming increasingly secularized and worldly-minded, all of us must be on our guard. We must beware of becoming prodigal sons, straying from our Father's house and despising his Holy Word. Every Saturday we should be eagerly anticipating the opportunity offered us the next day to go into the house of the Lord to gain more comfort, spiritual strength and guidance from God's Word. Indeed, every day we should gladly heed the psalmist David's invitation: "Taste and see that the LORD is good." If we truly trust in the Lord and are faithful children of our heavenly Father, we will never tire of tasting the rich, nourishing food we Christians find in God's Word, for the boundless grace of God in Jesus Christ is exactly the kind of bread we need to sustain our hungry souls.

Remember then, the Father's house here on earth is always open as usual, stocked to the ceiling with a rich supply of the true Bread, Jesus Christ. Don't ignore the Father's loving invitation. Come! Taste! See the goodness and free salvation of the Lord! Don't make the mistake of the prodigal son; don't choose the way of spiritual famine, for there's no denying that the famine of the Word is the worst judgment possible.

On Christ, the true Bread, let us feed,
Let Him to us be drink indeed,
And let us taste with joyfulness
The Holy Spirit's plenteousness. Amen.

Then the woman said to Elijah, "Now I know that you are a man of God and that the word of the LORD from your mouth is the truth." (1 Kings 17:24)

HIS WORD IS TRUTH

God promises mercy, not punishment. He promises that he will not deal with us according to our sins, but for Jesus' sake he will pardon and bless. He promises us unspeakable joy.

But will God keep those promises? Can we count on them? Or should we only take them figuratively? Do his words perhaps only mean that this is what he wishes for us, rather than this is what he will bring about for us?

How much do God's promises count when all we see is failure, and all we feel is despair? It may be easy to sing his praises in church on a bright Sunday morning. Can we do the same, will we do the same when our life seems so dark and depressing that we don't even care if the sun is shining or not?

We might say, "We will, if we have faith!" And that is correct. The writer of the Epistle to the Hebrews reminds us, "Now faith is being sure of what we hope for and certain of what we do not see." But thank God, what we Christians hope for and what we are certain of is not the product of our imagination or our efforts.

We have faith, but it is not blind faith. With St. Paul we can say, "I know whom I have believed." Our faith lays hold of the living God with whom all things are possible.

God has proven himself sufficiently in the past. Jesus came as the fulfillment of his promises. In him we already have all good things. The life, death and resurrection of Jesus are proof beyond all doubt that the promises of God are true. He is not just a God who talks. He is the Lord who acts.

The former heathen widow had come to learn that for herself. She had seen the proof with her own eyes. Now she knew for certain that Elijah was a man of God. But more importantly she knew that the word of the Lord that came from his prophet was the truth.

May we be reminded of this truth by her example. Believing when we cannot see and trusting when we cannot comprehend, may we cling to God's gracious promises. He even promises to give us the strength to do so. We need nothing more.

Eternal God, grant unto your servants the light from on high, so that our hearts and lives may reflect your glory. Amen.

But his delight is in the law of the LORD, and on his law he meditates day and night. (Psalm 1:2)

GOD'S WORD—THE SOURCE OF OUR JOY

The Bible reveals two great doctrines. One is the Law; the other is the Gospel. The Law is always Law and the Gospel is always Gospel. The two may never be mixed. They may never be confused. However, we must be aware that the Bible uses the expression, "the law of the Lord," not only to denote the doctrine of the Law, but in a broader sense, to point to both doctrines—the entire Word of God. That is what the expression, "law of the Lord" refers to in our psalm. That is the single source of true joy in this world. It is experienced when men find their delight in the Word of God.

Why is it that in this vale of tears so little joy and happiness is still sought in that Word of the Lord? Why, for instance, did the prodigal son rather seek his joy in spending his inheritance in a far country where he might live unnoticed, away from the influence of that Word? Why did he seek his joy in riotous living amid harlots, so that he finally ended his quest for happiness in being a guest of swine?

On the other hand, why is it that even among Christians the Bible, "the law of the Lord," is more and more becoming a closed book? Why are many restricting their reading to secular novels and magazines? They may be good ones, but these people let days and months pass without once opening the Law of the Lord.

One cause underlies this all. Bible reading does not come about naturally. By nature the imagination of man's heart is evil, and his mind is enmity against God. It reacts the same way against God's Word and finds no delight in it. Thus sin would cut us off from this source of joy.

Tenderly God coaxes us to turn to his Word as the source of our joy. He reminds us that his Word can make us wise to salvation. It brings us the righteousness of Christ to cover our sin and cheer our heart. It gives us a wondrous knowledge that makes us happier than gold ever could. It is sweeter than honey to our hearts. God would say, "Sinner, come regularly and take this treasure. Break off from this honeycomb and eat. Let your soul delight itself in my Word. It will bring you joy for time and for eternity."

Heavenly Father, teach me to love your sacred Word and view my Savior here. "Oh, may these heavenly pages be my ever dear delight; and still new beauties may I see and still increasing light!" Amen.

O LORD, you will keep us safe and protect us from such people forever. (Psalm 12:7)

HOLD FAST TO THE WORD

Defend Thy truth, O God, and stay
This evil generation;
And from the error of its way
Keep Thine own congregation.
The wicked everywhere abound
And would Thy little flock confound;
But Thou art our Salvation.

(TLH 260:6)

T his stanza of Luther's hymn is an earnest prayer that God would keep his congregation safe from the errors of this evil generation of arrogant false prophets. How timely this prayer is for this day and age in which we live! The wicked truly abound everywhere. False doctrine and practice surround us on every side. The little flock of those who hold fast to the full truth of God's Word seems hopelessly outnumbered.

Yet we need not despair. For the Lord is our Salvation. He will fight for us and keep us safe and secure, if we only hold fast to his Word. Think of Gideon and his 300 whom God sent to fight against the Midianite army of 135,000 (cf. Judges 7). They were certainly a little flock, an outwardly small and seemingly insignificant army with an impossible task. But God was with them and gave them the victory. Think of the three men in the fiery furnace (Daniel 3). Their situation also looked hopeless from a human point of view, and yet they, too, were delivered from the hand of the enemy by the Lord to whom they clung in humble faith. Or think of St. Paul. He stood almost as one man against the world in his missionary activity for Christ. Trusting in the Lord, his Strength and Salvation, he conquered the heathen world for the Savior.

And so also shall we, by God's grace, overcome and obtain the victory. For, though taking a firm stand for the truth and against all that is not in full agreement with that truth will mean standing in the minority, yet we shall not be standing alone. For then we shall have the Lord on our side and have nothing to fear, for as St. Paul assures us: "If God is for us, who can be against us?" (Romans 8:31)

May we, then, in these last days of sore distress, hold fast to the Lord our Salvation and to his Word of truth, confident that he will bless us and keep us and bring us safely to our eternal home above!

Oh, grant that in Thy holy Word
We here may live and die, dear Lord;
And when our journey endeth here,
Receive us into glory there. Amen.

Now what I am commanding you today is not too difficult for you or beyond your reach. (Deuteronomy 30:11)

THE WORD IN NEED

Needs and wants are not always distinguished. We may want things we do not need such as possessions, wealth and success. We may also need things we do not want such as punishment, correction or trials. During our lifetime we can count on times of varying needs. We never know what each day will bring, but we live in the constant assurance that the Lord will supply our every need. He does this according to his superior wisdom. He also does this according to his gracious promises. He is never far from us in his word, never beyond our reach.

What are our needs? Has health suddenly deteriorated to a point where our accustomed lifestyle has been severely limited? Psalm 73:26 is near to remind us, "My flesh and my heart may fail, but God is the strength of my heart and my portion forever."

Are the problems piled so high that joy seems to be gone from life? James 1:12 states, "Blessed is the man who perseveres under trial, because when he has stood the test, he will receive the crown of life that God promised to those who love him."

Is our need perhaps a correction because we have brought on our own misery? In the words of Proverbs 28:13 God reminds us, "He who conceals his sins does not prosper, but whoever confesses and renounces them finds mercy."

Are we worried about the future? Have we forgotten the message of Romans 8:32, "He who did not spare his own Son, but gave him up for us all—how will he not also, along with him, graciously give us all things?" Yes, truly, in his Word "the Lord is near to all who call on him in truth."

It is not fitting for a child of God to bemoan his lot in life or to despair of help. We have a heavenly Father who knows us by name. We are members of his family of believers through Jesus Christ. He watches over us and supplies what we need. He does not give us everything we want as a wise father knows is best. But he also does not leave us without help in time of need.

We are not alone and adrift on a stormy sea. We are on the way to the bright shores of heaven where there is no pain, sorrow or need. Our path here is lighted by God's sure Word. Turn to it and see the way through each and every trial, test and temptation.

**Grant, Lord, that from your Word we learn
The wisdom it imparts
And to its heavenly teaching turn
With simple, childlike hearts. Amen.**

The grass withers and the flowers fall, but the word of our God stands forever." (Isaiah 40:8)

THE ETERNAL WORD

If human wisdom and strength were all we had on which to build our lives and hopes, we would be miserable creatures indeed. We would spend our lives in a frantic rush to get as much as we could of what the world has to offer. We would regard every setback as a tragedy. We would have a dreadful fear of death and a sense of complete hopelessness about any future life. We would have no lasting comfort, peace or joy. In tones as solemn as the tolling of the funeral bell Isaiah repeats the unfailing truth that summarizes all of human life, "All men are like grass . . . the grass withers and the flowers fall." How true are the hymnwriter's words, "Change and decay in all around I see."

What a glorious comfort to be reassured by the Lord himself that there is something more important and lasting than the powers and possessions of the world. What a comfort to hear that in a world of death and decay, there is something which lives and abides forever. That something is the Word of God in the Holy Scripture. By the Word of the Lord the world was made. By his Word of power all things are upheld. And by the Living Word hearts are turned from sin to forgiveness and life in Jesus Christ. This Word of God does not change. And it will abide forever.

Those who anchor their faith and hope in the Word will not be put to shame. Trusting in the Word and its promises, believers face the future unafraid. Life's tragedies and reverses do not disturb them. Daily the Word assures them of forgiveness of sins, peace with God and eternal joy. To Israel, God's promises provided the comfort of forgiveness and deliverance. Today that same Word still speaks comfort and peace personally to each of us.

Ask any pastor, and he will tell you that the greatest joy of his ministry is the privilege of bringing the unchanging Word of God, the one thing that really matters, to people in every condition. The eternal Word brings forgiveness to troubled sinners young and old, peace to those searching for the meaning of life, comfort to the sick and hope to the dying. Nor is sharing the Word the privilege of pastors only. Christ has given his Word to all believers, a precious trust to have and to share until his return. May we all ever cling to, abide in and gladly share the eternal Word of Truth!

Preserve among us, O Lord, the treasure of your abiding Word. Amen.

Then the woman said to Elijah, "Now I know that you are a man of God and that the word of the LORD from your mouth is the truth." (1 Kings 17:24)

THE WORD OF THE PROPHETS IS THE WORD OF THE LORD

After Elijah appeared before Ahab and proclaimed a judgment upon Israel by famine and drought, God had him hide by the brook Cherith where ravens brought him food. God then sent him to a widow of Zarephath in Sidon. When he arrived, she was gathering firewood. He asked her for a drink. As she went to get some water, he said, "And bring me, please, a piece of bread."

"As surely as the LORD your God lives," she replied, "I don't have any bread—only a handful of flour in a jar and a little oil in a jug. I am gathering a few sticks to take home and make a meal for myself and my son, that we may eat it—and die."

Elijah said to her, "Don't be afraid. Go home and do as you have said. But first make a small cake of bread for me from what you have and bring it to me, and then make something for yourself and your son. For this is what the LORD, the God of Israel, says: 'The jar of flour will not be used up and the jug of oil will not run dry until the day the LORD gives rain on the land.' " The woman did so, and Elijah stayed with them throughout the famine without the flour or oil failing.

Everything seemed secure and happy when suddenly the widow's son became ill and died. The widow, blinded by grief, said to Elijah, "What do you have against me, man of God?" Elijah said, "Give me your son." He carried him upstairs to his bedroom, laid him on his bed, and prayed, "O LORD my God, have you brought tragedy also upon this widow I am staying with, by causing her son to die?" Then he stretched himself out on the boy three times and cried to the LORD, "O LORD my God, let this boy's life return to him!"

God heard the prayer of Elijah and restored the child to life. Elijah took him to his mother and said, "Look, your son is alive!" With heartfelt joy she said, "Now I know that you are a man of God and that the word of the LORD from your mouth is the truth."

For both Elijah and the widow this experience became one of great comfort and blessing. It assured them of God's love and abiding presence. It thus prepared them for the future. Our crosses and trials will do likewise if in them we turn to God in faith for help. Through them God wants to help us make him the center of our life and to hope in his love and mercy. Our faith will be helped through them to enable us to say with the widow, "Now I know . . . that the Word of the Lord . . . is truth. I know that all of Scripture, all of its promises are true. They are mine, and nobody can take them from me."

May we, by God's grace, come to live in this certainty of faith through our crosses or trials! In this confidence of faith we will then ever be ready for tomorrow and tomorrow and tomorrow until we finally rest in the "golden tomorrow." God grant us this for Jesus' sake.

Lord, let me know your Word as the truth, both now and forever. Amen.

In you, O LORD, I have taken refuge; let me never be put to shame; deliver me in your righteousness. (Psalm 31:1)

FAITH GROUNDED IN THE WORD

In Thee, Lord, have I put my trust;
Leave me not helpless in the dust,
Let me not be confounded.
Let in Thy Word My faith, O Lord,
Be always firmly grounded.

(TLH 524:1)

The Bible has a message for every condition and circumstance of human life. There are always such among us as have been called to walk in the vale of suffering and sorrow, troubles and tears. For them the Thirty-First Psalm brings a word of comfort, cheer and strength

It is also a word for you who have thus far been spared the cup of suffering, a word that will bring strong consolation and uphold you when trouble does come. If you are a true child of God, you will be beaten and battered by enmity, hatred and ridicule from without, and by fear and trembling from within. But here is divine counsel as to how a Christian is to deport himself in the time of trouble: not murmur, or complain or find fault with God, but trust and pray.

Christianity does not guarantee immunity. A Christian is not exempt from things that hit and hurt. For the Christian, too, life can be extremely frustrating and frightening.

Why do troubles come to the children of God? Sometimes there is a superficial answer given to this question by the unregenerate smart-aleck critic who pounces upon the Christian and says: "This trouble is no doubt the result of some sin on your part." But the Word of God is not that cruel. Christ says: "As many as I love, I rebuke and chasten." It is part of the plan, program and purpose of your life to suffer trials and troubles. "We must go through many hardships to enter the kingdom of God."

Troubles are designed to test us and teach us to trust. Trust in the Word of God is the lesson of the first verse of our psalm: In him we find refuge and rest, safety and security; we shall never be confounded or put to shame and thereby bring shame and disgrace upon him in whom we trust. God is righteous and faithful. He will keep the promises of the covenant he made with David and with us.

Then follow the admonition given by the Christian poet:

Leave all to His direction;
In wisdom He doth reign,
And in a way most wondrous
His course He will maintain.
Soon He, His promise keeping,
With wonder-working skill
Shall put away the sorrows
That now thy spirit fill.

(TLH 520:8)

Hear our prayer, O Lord; in your faithfulness answer us, and in your righteousness deliver us. Amen.

He makes springs pour water into the ravines; it flows between the mountains. They give water to all the beasts of the field; the wild donkeys quench their thirst. The birds of the air nest by the waters; they sing among the branches. He waters the mountains from his upper chambers; the earth is satisfied by the fruit of his work. He makes grass grow for the cattle, and plants for man to cultivate—bringing forth food from the earth: wine that gladdens the heart of man, oil to make his face shine, and bread that sustains his heart. (Psalm 104:10-15)

OUR FATHER PROVIDES FOR ALL

The psalmist paints a peaceful and beautiful word-picture for us, a pastoral scene which would be worth reading even if it were not the inspired Word of God saying something special to the family of God. It is a picture of wild and domestic animals, wild grasses and cereal crops, the birds of the air and man the earth-dweller. There is water and air, hill and valley, green and blue. There are the three main products of the Mediterranean world: grapes, olives, and wheat—a delicious picture. All of it is saying: God is a thoughtful and generous Provider. He gives basic nourishment and he adds all the good things of life to it.

He is the Provider of what we all "natural resources." The minerals used for the girders of skyscrapers and the gears of farm machinery and the gauges of delicate instruments — these were placed in the earth for man's use by God's bounty. The wealth of the forest, and the ability to use wood products in an endless variety of ways—these have come from the generosity of the heavenly Provider. The barely investigated wealth of the sea, where each drop of water is a busy world all by itself—the Creator has made it.

In the beginning God spoke and it was so, and it is still so. He speaks and things happen, and they keep on happening. The rich variety of life in the world, the abundant food supplies which do not fail (though man fails in the use of them), the cycle of life and death and regeneration in the creature world—these are evidences that God's creating Word is still effective.

He provides for the least of his creatures in order to preserve his highest creature — man. In the words of Luther, he is "richly and daily providing clothing and shoes, meat and drink, house and home, wife and children, land, cattle, and all my goods, and all that I need to keep my body and life."

Heavenly Father, for all your benefits and bounty, it is our duty to thank and praise and to serve and obey you. As your Son has freed us from sin to serve you, let this duty be our highest joy. Amen.

These all look to you to give them their food at the proper time. When you give it to them, they gather it up; when you open your hand, they are satisfied with good things. When you hide your face, they are terrified; when you take away their breath, they die and return to the dust. When you send your Spirit, they are created, and you renew the face of the earth. (Psalm 104:27-30)

ALL DEPENDS ON OUR FATHER

Some people take the attitude: "God is too great, too busy, too remote, to be interested in me personally." That might be a complaint. It might be false humility. It might be wishful thinking on the part of someone who has a bad conscience and hopes that God is not interested in what he does. But we should not measure God by our standards nor judge him by our limitations. He is God, and so his eye can be on the sparrow and his mind can number the very hairs of our heads. He does not lose sight of our best interests or neglect our needs. He is vitally interested in what we do with the gift of life.

The continued existence of all things depends on the Father-Creator. The seeds which the sparrow eats, the food of the fish in the sea, the crops which men harvest and the food we gather into baskets at the supermarket come from his generous hand. The food itself, the strength to gather it, the ability of our bodies to turn that food into energy and strength are all gifts of his goodness. He is not too great to care about these things. At the wedding of Cana, Jesus did not refuse to provide wine on the basis that he had more important things to do—like redeeming the world. So the Father does not refuse to give any further attention to the creature world on the ground that he is busy gathering the Church from the great mass of sinners.If he should close his hand or turn his face, there would be no life on this earth. Even those who deny his preserving care could not draw another breath without his power and care. Those who refuse to look to him or acknowledge their dependence on him could not live another moment if he were not such a dependable God. The same Spirit who moved over the face of the waters and changed chaos to cosmos is still lending the breath of life to all things, including mankind. Each spring, each renewing of the earth, is evidence of his life-giving ways. It is the same Spirit who teaches us that this is our Father's world and enables us to appreciate that we can also depend on him for eternal life in Jesus Christ, who has taught us to call the Creator and Preserver "Father."

Almighty Father, send your Spirit upon us in rich measure, that we may appreciate and receive with thanksgiving our daily bread. Amen.

You covered it with the deep as with a garment; the waters stood above the mountains. But at your rebuke the waters fled, at the sound of your thunder they took to flight; they flowed over the mountains, they went down into the valleys, to the place you assigned for them. You set a boundary they cannot cross; never again will they cover the earth. (Psalm 104:6-9).

OUR FATHER GOVERNS THE WORLD

We are missing very much in life if we are not interested in the wonders of nature which surround us. Curiosity about the "laws" of nature is part of our humanity, and when we have been made whole in Christ that curiosity is part of our sanctified lives. So we study and respect the balance of nature, the ways in which the multitude of plants and animals depend on one another. We consider the glory of a field of flowers or the mystery of a single flower. We observe the ants and bees with their wonderful organized activity. We read about and watch the marvelous, ordered and predictable ways of the stars and planets. We know about the uniqueness and beauty of each snowflake, the leaf systems of the trees. We confess as the psalmist did: "In wisdom you have made them all."

What keeps it all in order? Not our clever minds! "You set a boundary," says the psalmist. God has established the place and the function of everything in his world. When the earth was "formless and empty. . . . God said, 'Let the water under the sky be gathered to one place, and let dry ground appear: and it was so.' " It was so and it is so. The man who wrote the psalm had the story of Creation in mind. What God had established in the beginning still held true when he wrote. It still holds true today. We observe nature and say, "That's the way things are; that's the way they have to be." But the reason they are that way and can be depended upon to remain that way is that in the beginning "God said."

And you are more important to him than all other creatures. To which of his other creatures has he said: "Have dominion over my creation"? With which of his other creatures does he converse as he converses with us by addressing us in his Word and hearing our prayers? To which of his creatures does he come with the invitation to be his children and heirs of his glory? "The earth is the Lord's, and the fulness thereof," but you are doubly his, for he has also redeemed you at tremendous cost to himself. In Christ Jesus he has restored order to your life by imputing the righteousness of the Holy One to you.

Almighty God, continue to protect, guide and govern your creation. Amen.

As a father has compassion on his children, so the LORD has compassion on those who fear him; for he knows how we are formed, he remembers that we are dust. (Psalm 103:13,14)

OUR FATHER'S HEART

Within two months, death claimed a son and daughter of Daniel Webster. Edward, said that father, was "my heart's delight," and Julia was Edward's "angel sister." The sorrowing father planted two elm trees in his yard in their memory.

Charles Dickens saw his youngest son, just 16, off for Australia. The author-father wrote to a friend, "It was a hard parting . . . he seemed to become once more my youngest and favorite little child . . . I did not think I could have been so shaken."

Abraham loved his son Isaac. With a father's grieving heart he dutifully bound the boy and, at God's command, prepared to sacrifice him.

David's son Absalom tried to steal his father's throne. For it, he was put to death. When David heard it, he went up into a little room over the city gate and, with many tears, wished he had died in his son's place.

Our text uses this example of a father's love to teach us an important truth about God. Our Lord has a great affection for "those who fear him." God is full of pity toward all men, especially toward those who believe in his Son. The reason? "He knows how we are formed; he remembers that we are dust."

Who should know our "frame" better than God! Whether we eat, sleep, work or play, you and I are animated dust. One psalm says that God "planted the ear" and "formed the eye," and the writer of another says to God, "Your hands made me and fashioned me." We are dust-people. We live in dust-bodies. At death the richest and poorest among us again turn to dust.

God knows how weak and frail we really are. Because he pities us, he sent his Son to take on a dust body and, in that body, to pay for the sins of our lost, helpless world. Our Father pities us in our guilt and pronounces us clean in Christ Jesus. He pities us in our troubles and promises to hear our prayers. Because our Father remembers that we are dust, with mortal hearts pulsing in our breasts, he sends his Spirit to strengthen, guide and cheer us.

Why this tenderness, this sympathy? Look inside God's heart! Our Father "has compassion on his children."

Gracious God, continue to pour out upon us the sympathy that fills your fatherly heart. Do it for Jesus' sake. Amen.

The Lord is compassionate and gracious, slow to anger, abounding in love. He will not always accuse, nor will he harbor his anger forever; he does not treat us as our sins deserve or repay us according to our iniquities. For as high as the heavens are above the earth, so great is his love for those who fear him; as far as the east is from the west, so far has he removed our transgressions from us. (Psalm 103:8-12)

OUR FATHER'S MERCY

A German submarine sank a British freighter off Africa in 1941. The sub surfaced amid wreckage, lifeboats and wounded men. When the British were ordered to board the sub, they thought they would be killed or captured. Instead the German captain had his doctor treat their wounds. His crewmen repaired their lifeboats. He gave them food, water, wine and tobacco, then set them on a course for the nearest land.

After the war, one of the British survivors sought out the kind-hearted German captain and invited him to be his guest in England. He was grateful for that wartime act of mercy.

David exults in these verses over God's great mercy to sinners. By the inspiration of the Spirit, he lets us look into God's heart-of-hearts where we see nothing but love, grace and mercy.

You and I should not be permitted to read words like these! We have waged open warfare against God. The grave should swallow us, and we should sink into a sea of torment forever. Jeremiah included us when he wrote, "We lie down in our shame . . . we have sinned against the Lord our God."

Has today been spoiled for you by some new, fresh sin? Does the spectacle of all your life's sin look to you like hell on parade? Does your conscience shout at you until you want to hold your ears? Then go stand by David while he blesses the Lord! Listen while he proclaims the sweetest truth we will ever hear!

God has not dealt with us after our sins. He put our sins on Christ and *dealt with Christ*. He rewarded Christ according to our iniquities. Jesus' *reward* was the bitterness of our hell, a cup of suffering and the cross. But when his awful work was done, Jesus had removed our transgressions as far out of God's sight as east is from west! In God's eyes, we have no sin! The warfare is over. God, plenteous in mercy, has bound our wounds. He has provisioned us with Christ's own holiness. By his Spirit he has set us on a course for heaven.

I thank Thee, O God, for your mercy toward me, a sinner. Amen.

The LORD make his face shine upon you and be gracious to you. (Numbers 6:25)

OUR FATHER'S FACE

S unshine. Most everybody loves it. In winter months northerners like to travel south to get away from the cold and take in some sunshine. The bright sunshine symbolizes warmth, life and happiness. No wonder people love it. But the sun isn't the only thing that makes us happy when it shines. People do too. When someone is very excited or glad, we say that his face lights up.We love to see it happen. It's contagious. Before we know it, we're smiling along with that person. If it's good when other people smile at us, think of how fantastic it is when God's face lights up and he smiles at us.

By every right we shouldn't expect him to be happy with us. We've done much more to make God frown than smile. Sometimes the Bible talks about God's expression toward sin. The picture then is not of a shining face. Scripture declares, "The face of the Lord is against those who do evil." Certainly we are among "those who do evil." Yet God would much rather smile on us. And he does smile on us every day as he blesses us with schools, churches, homes, family, friends, food, clothing and ten thousand other gifts. He smiles as he blesses us with his Word and sacraments, with forgiveness, life and salvation.

Why does God's face shine toward us? Because of Jesus, "the Sun of righteousness." When he was on the cross, Jesus took our sins up there with him and suffered God's anger in our place. Now God sees us, not as filthy sinners who deserve nothing but punishment, but as his precious children. It was because he looked forward to the joy of saving sinners like us that Jesus the Son of God endured the cross.

This shining love of God is contagious. It lights up our faces and makes us want to smile at others. God loves us. Though at times his bright face may be hidden behind the clouds, we know it hasn't changed. His love remains the same —yesterday, today and forever.

The sun may shine brightly in the sky, but not nearly so brightly as the face of God. Doesn't that make us smile, even if we can't go south for the winter?

God of mercy, God of grace,
Show the brightness of Thy face;
Shine upon us, Savior shine;
Fill Thy church with light divine,
And Thy saving health extend
Unto earth's remotest end. Amen.

The Lord said to Satan, "Very well, then, everything he has is in your hands, but on the man himself do not lay a finger." (Job 1:12)

OUR FATHER IS IN CONTROL

How can there be a just God, with so much misery and suffering in this world? The Scriptures assure us that the Lord reigns. They tell us that Satan is conquered. Yet he seems to have so much power.

Satan is the prince of this world, Satan does go about as a roaring lion seeking whom he may devour. He still does inflict misery and suffering upon his hapless victims whenever and however he can. But he is not without limits.

"But on the man himself do not lay a finger." Here God did set a limit. Satan could do so much and no more. This scene in heaven was hidden from faithful Job. When suffering struck him on earth, he could only ask why and what next. Satan attacked Job with all the forces at his command. But still the Lord overruled the purposes of Satan, so that Job would not be tempted above what he was able to bear.

This hidden transaction in heaven is like the beginning of a drama. Behind the curtain the scenery and props are all in place. The actors take their positions. All the lighting is adjusted just right. And the audience can see none of this until the curtain is finally lifted.

For us God lifts the curtain before we read of the suffering of Job and gives us a glimpse of his heavenly plan. He shows us that he will not allow Satan to pass the limits which he himself sets. He shows us that his only purpose in allowing all this agony is to strengthen and purify Job, and to make the glory of his faith shine with even greater brilliance as he bears his adversity in patience.

Job couldn't see all this. He had to walk by faith, not by sight. And so must we all. If Job had to look around and could not see any end to his suffering, and could look only to the coming Redeemer who would liberate him, we too must confess that the plans of God are dark for us and that faith in Christ is our only light.

God in heaven still limits Satan, so that no matter how hard he tries he cannot do us permanent harm. The whole Book of Revelation shows us the Church suffering and persecuted here on earth, but with a glorious future assured her in heaven.

Job suffered. He didn't always know why. We suffer too. And we can't always see why. But we can be sure of this, that as we suffer with Christ, we shall also be glorified with him. God is still in charge, and he is still the loving Savior.

Lord, lead us to trust that your love still controls our ways. Amen.

Who has measured the waters in the hollow of his hand, or with the breadth of his hand marked off the heavens? Who has held the dust of the earth in a basket, or weighed the mountains on the scales and the hills in a balance? (Isaiah 40:12)

OUR FATHER'S POWER

How much water can you hold in the palm of your hand? How much of the dust of the earth could you take up with a scoop? How would you weigh a mountain? Our limitations, however, are not God's. God measured the waters with his palm. He laid out the universe. He formed the earth and established the size of its mountains.

He is Creator, Preserver—the Almighty God.

At the time Isaiah wrote these words the return of the people of Israel to their homeland seemed impossible. Because human reason said that such a thing was impossible, many concluded that this was also something that God could not accomplish. With the words of this text, God through Isaiah reminded his people that in their thinking they ought not limit God to that which is humanly possible.

Just because we cannot make something out of nothing does not indicate that God cannot do so. Just because it is hard for us to conceive of a flood so great that it covered all the earth does not mean that God could not bring about such a deluge. How wonderful that God's power is vastly superior to ours! Thus he can solve our problems, heal our illnesses, provide for our needs and even make evil work for our good. Because of God's omnipotence we need not fear. "Therefore we will not fear, though the earth give way and the mountains fall into the heart of the sea, though its waters roar and foam and the mountains quake with their surging" (Psalm 46:2,3).

St. Paul wrote, "I am not ashamed of the gospel, because it is the power of God for the salvation of everyone who believes"(Rom. 1:16). The Gospel of Christ, the Good News that he is our Savior, is the power of God that turned us from unbelief to saving faith. For this power, which also sustains our faith, we ought daily to thank God.

Scripture tells us that it was Abraham who "Against all hope . . . in hope believed . . . being fully persuaded that God had power to do what he had promised" (Romans 4:18,21). Abraham believed God's promises because he knew that God could do vastly more than that which is possible for man to accomplish. Abraham believed that "The Lord God OMNIPOTENT reigneth."

Lord, I believe. Help mine unbelief. Amen.

Lord, I have heard of your fame; I stand in awe of your deeds, O Lord. Renew them in our day in our time make them known. (Habakkuk 3:2)

OUR FATHER'S FAME ENDURES

A few decades ago one of the popular songs regularly heard on the radio was the Ballad of Davy Crockett. The song related the legendary exploits and heroic deeds of the early American frontiersman. Davy Crockett was larger than life to the youngsters who delighted to hear about his amazing strength and fantastic accomplishments. But feats of Davy Crockett or of any other hero, real or legendary, are nothing in comparison with the real deeds of the Lord God Almighty.

Habakkuk, the prophet, had learned about the Lord's deeds, and he stood in awe of them. Habakkuk had heard how the Lord created the earth and the universe and everything in them in six days. He had heard how the Lord sent a great flood to destroy the world and all the people in it except Noah and his family. Habakkuk had heard how the Lord delivered the people of Israel from the Egyptians by parting the waters of the Red Sea and drowning the soldiers of Egypt in the sea. Habakkuk stood in awe of what the Lord had done, and he prayed that the Lord would lead his contemporaries to understand and to appreciate his mighty deeds too.

How awe-struck are you by what the Lord has done? It's so easy to forget or to fail fully to appreciate the Lord's great deeds. Often we find ourselves more impressed by man's feeble accomplishments. We need seriously to reflect on the awesome deeds of the Lord in the past. We also need to stand in awe of God's deeds performed all around us every day. We should remember who makes the sun to shine, the rain to fall, the crops to grow; who placed the power in the atom; who sustains and preserves the lives of all his creatures. It is God who guides and governs men and nations. It is God the Holy Ghost who works the miracle of faith in every believer's heart.

The most awesome of all God's deeds was when he sent his one and only Son into this world to assume our human nature. He lived a perfect life on behalf of all mankind. He took upon himself the sins of all people of all time and endured God's wrath in our stead so that we might be saved eternally. This is the deed we pray he would continue to make known through us to all the people in the world.

We stand in awe of your deeds, O Lord. Cause the good news of your love and salvation in Jesus to fill my heart and the hearts of people everywhere with awe and praise for you, in Jesus' name. Amen.

"Lift up your eyes and look about you: All assemble and come to you; your sons come from afar, and your daughters are carried on the arm." (Isaiah 60:4)

OUR FATHER'S GLORY

What has God been doing about conditions in the world today? This is a question scoffers ask so often of faithful Christians. Indeed, sometimes the problems of this world in which we live seem to overwhelm us; sometimes God seems to be so far away. We live in an age of economic and political unrest, to be sure. But let us not permit either this or the muttering of the prophets of doom to cause us to go about our daily lives with eyes downcast in despair.

Just what is God doing? Let us heed the words of the prophet Isaiah, "Lift up your eyes and look about you." All right, let us look up from our troubles. What shall we see? Wars and political crises? Crime? An impending energy crisis? No! The prophet is not directing us to look upon the mess that sinful mankind has made of this world. We find no comfort there.

Let us today look where the prophet would have us direct our eyes, to the family of God. Let us see the people who are coming to the Light of the world in faith. These are precious souls redeemed by the saving work of Jesus.

God's family is called the Church. Each Sunday we confess in the words of the Apostles' Creed: "I believe in the holy Christian Church, the communion of saints." Let us believe in our hearts what we confess with our mouths.

Jesus has come, and by God's grace you believe in him as your only Savior. You are God's sons and daughters. Yes, children of God, lift up your eyes! See the blessings that are yours both now in this life and for all eternity. But you are not alone.

What is God doing? While the world trembles in the throes of sin and with the fear of destruction, God is quietly carrying out his plan of salvation through the still, small voice of his gospel. Daily the family to which we belong, the communion of saints, is growing. And what a wonderful family it is! It knows no cultural, racial or national barriers or boundaries. Membership in this family is based solely upon faith in Jesus Christ as one's personal Savior.

Let us look up and see what God is doing. People the world over are hearing and by God's grace are believing the gospel. God has not forgotten us. His kingdom is being enlarged daily through the power of his Holy Spirit.

Lord, we thank you for the grace you have shown us and all your children. Amen.

Do you not know? Have you not heard? The Lord is the everlasting God, the Creator of the ends of the earth. He will not grow tired or weary, and his understanding no one can fathom. (Isaiah 40:28)

HE WATCHES OVER US DAY AND NIGHT

To *know* God in the truest sense of the word is to believe him and trust in him under all circumstances, no matter how trying. Israel in its misery had forgotten God and failed to remember what he could do. Thus, in their despair, the people of Israel feared they were out of reach of God's help.

There are many daily difficulties that we face that tend to discourage and depress us. The boring routine of work has father wishing the weekend were already here. Mother can't make the budget stretch to feed and clothe the family, and company is coming. The children are rowdy, and they must be reminded again and again to do even the simplest of their chores. But is this all so strange? Is not this exactly what God told Adam and Eve that life would be like when they had fallen into sin? (See Genesis 3:16-19)

Our troubles are not because God does not know what is going on, or because he is tired and sleeping while we suffer. The very opposite is true. He does know, and he carefully watches over us day and night. Our problem is our own sinful nature.

And part of our sinful nature is forgetfulness.

Today's Scripture verse is a call for us to remember who God is. He is everlasting, that is, he has always been and will always continue to exist. Also, he is the Creator. Don't ever let any evolutionistic idea rob you of that truth. For to lose sight of God as Creator is to forget that he is Lord, that is, in full command of heaven and earth.

Remember also the past. To be sure, there have been problems and hard times. But our God has always sustained us. If that were not true, not one of us would be alive today.

Finally, look to the future. God has a great salvation prepared for us. Through a plan so simple, yet so far beyond our understanding, God placed our sin on his Son. He permitted his Son, Jesus Christ, to die the death of the cross so that by faith (trust) in him we might have life eternal as a free gift. To keep us in this faith, God graciously watches over us every moment of every day and night. Let no one say that God is asleep or that he doesn't care.

Lord, my Shepherd, I shall not want. I will fear no evil for you are with me. Surely goodness and mercy shall be mine forever. Amen.

Therefore the law is paralyzed, and justice never prevails. The wicked hem in the righteous, so that justice is perverted. (Habakkuk 1:4)

GOD IS IN CONTROL

"The way things are going in this life it appears that God has lost control. It appears that Satan is ruling. There doesn't seem to be any hope for anything." These are the thoughts and words of some depressed Christians.

This world does seem out of control. It appears that criminals are well off and honest people are losing their shirts. It appears that the unscrupulous are immorally using legalities to free the guilty and oppress the innocent. The laws seem paralyzed and unable to help the downtrodden. It seems that wicked people are in control and justice is perverted. The days we are living in and the times of Habakkuk appear to have many similarities.

In these days of frustration we ought to remember that "our God is in heaven: he does whatever pleases him." God allows people to reject his love and bring destruction upon themselves and others. He does not force people to believe in him and serve him. Yet history is "his story." God is in control. He is with his believers and will deliver them from evil.

God causes good to come to the Christians in the days of trouble. Evil days move us to look more frequently to God for help. Oppression and affliction force us to exercise our faith. In the dark days of injustice we have opportunity to let the light of Christ shine brightly in our daily life.

Our God will never test our faith beyond our ability to endure afflictions. He will give us the strength to bear every burden. He will allow evil to go only so far and then will deliver his people. Human laws are often paralyzed, and human justice is often perverted. Our God's law is not paralyzed or his justice perverted. He is almighty to save, and his ways are more than just.

Satan and evil people may be allowed to take our earthly treasures. But they cannot take away the forgiveness and eternal life Jesus earned for us. Nothing but our own unbelief can rob us of the love and salvation of God. Our God is in control and will make all things work together for the good of those who trust in him.

Our Father, deliver us from evil, for the kingdom and the power and the glory are yours forever and ever. Amen.

Praise be to the name of God for ever and ever; wisdom and power are his. He changes times and seasons; he sets up kings and deposes them. He gives wisdom to the wise and knowledge to the discerning. (Daniel 2:20,21)

IN GOD'S HANDS

God is always in control. He may allow killing frosts to come to Florida two years in a row. He may allow floods to rampage along the Ohio River valley. He may turn much of Africa into a desert. It may seem that nature is going out of control, but God is always in control. He still changes the seasons and provides the earth with "seedtime and harvest."

God is also in control of the people of this earth, even the great kings and leaders. They are like puppets on a string. They may rage and fume, but they can go no farther than God allows. Nebuchadnezzar, the King of Babylon, thought that he was high and mighty. But in the same day that he boasted of his greatness, Nebuchadnezzar was deprived of his sanity. God reduced his mental powers to those of a wild beast. Later God restored Nebuchadnezzar's sanity, and the king confessed that this humiliation was necessary so that he might know God and honor him.

Belshazzar, his successor to the throne, did not learn his lesson. He dared to defile the sacred vessels that had been confiscated from the temple in Jerusalem. He and his wives and concubines used them to toast the false gods of Babylon. Belshazzar saw the original "handwriting on the wall." It prophesied Belshazzar's death and the destruction of Babylon. It happened that very night, because Belshazzar dared to despise the true God.

Believers can say confidently with another king, King David, "My times are in your hands." The only reason David became king of Israel was because God chose him and set him on his throne. As he looked back, David acknowledged the special goodness God had shown him.

God controls our lives in the same way as he did King David's. He has shown us his goodness and mercy. He has shown himself worthy of our trust. We do not have to look to men for guidance. We do not have to fear what evil men may do to us. We have the sure Word of God—God's unfailing wisdom and love are revealed in the Bible. There God reveals himself to us in Christ and leads us to eternal glory. We are in very good hands—God's hands.

Thou art the Life; the rending tomb
Proclaims Thy conqu'ring arm;
And those who put their trust in Thee
Nor death nor hell shall harm. Amen.

Nathan replied, "The Lᴏʀᴅ has taken away your sin. You are not going to die."(2 Samuel 12:13)

WHAT COMFORT—SIN FORGIVEN!

The Bible is a very truthful book. It presents God's people to us just as they are. It shows us the children of God in their triumphs and victories. It shows us the children of God in their failures and sins. It is a sad thing for us to watch David, this great king, this man after God's own heart, brought down into the dust to cry out, "I have sinned against the Lord." Yet it is all there for a reason. The Bible says that these things were written in order that we might learn from them.

David's double sin of adultery and murder was great indeed. It is hard to imagine two more terrible sins against God and man than these. However, we learn from our text that David was forgiven for what he had done. No sooner had David confessed with all his heart and soul, "I have sinned against the Lord," than the prophet replied, "The Lord has taken away your sin. You are not going to die."

How can this be? If God is just and righteous and if God is serious about his commandments, how can God forgive David's sin and not punish him for it? The answer is found in the death of our Lord Jesus Christ on the cross. Jesus took David's sins upon himself and paid the penalty David deserved. Jesus suffered the punishment that David so justly merited. For the sake of Jesus Christ, Nathan could say to David, "The Lord has taken away your sin."

But how can this be? Jesus had not even been born when David sinned. No matter. With God there is no past or future. He sees all things as present. He saw David's sins and at the same time the all-atoning sacrifice of Jesus for the sins of the whole world. David not only confessed his sins, but he also had faith in the precious promise of God to send a Savior into the world. David's faith in that Savior assured him that his sins were truly forgiven.

What a blessed comfort this is to us! We too have sinned against God and have deserved nothing from him but his wrath and punishment. For Jesus' sake God forgives. He forgave David his sins of adultery and murder. He forgave Paul his sins of persecution against the church of Christ. He forgave Peter his threefold denial of the Lord. Best of all, God forgives us.

Jesus, redeem, restore, forgive us through your precious blood. As heirs of our home in heaven we praise our pardoning God. Amen.

I am with you and will watch over you wherever you go, and I will bring you back to this land. I will not leave you until I have done what I have promised you." (Genesis 28:15)

ALWAYS AT OUR SIDE

People on the move. That is pretty much the story of our society today. But it's also the story of many a biblical character. Think how God called Abraham to make a move that would change his whole life. God called Abraham from Ur of the Chaldees to a land he had never seen before. Later, Israel moved from Egypt to the Promised Land. Later yet Israel made the journey to Babylon as captives and returned home safely. Jesus moved from place to place in Palestine preaching the Gospel. St. Paul and the rest of the apostles were no strangers to far travels, either.

We Christians live in a very mobile world. About one out of every five people move to a different location every year. People move looking for new jobs. Companies transfer their workers. People move to get a new outlook on life or to escape the past. Some move for reasons of health. Others for reasons of ease, retirement or careers.

Jacob decided to move to avoid the anger of his brother Esau. Remember, Jacob tricked his father to give him the best inheritance. This made Esau angry enough to kill Jacob. But Jacob left home, probably with a guilt-laden conscience, to seek his security and livelihood at his uncle Laban's, far away from home.

It wasn't an easy move for Jacob. As a boy, he loved his home. He was favored by his mother. Packing his belongings meant leaving his homeland. He was leaving the land which God promised to him and his descendants. Maybe he thought to himself, "Am I doing the right thing?"

How wonderful was the promise that came to him from heaven on the first night of his journey! The Lord said to Jacob, "I am with you. I will protect you wherever you go. I will bring you back to this land someday, and I will not leave you until I have done all that I promised." What a comfort to Jacob!

What a comfort for every believer! We cannot run away from God's presence. He is always in control, even though we attempt to fashion our own destiny. Who knows where we might move to in our lifetime? Remember, wherever we are, the Lord is at our side to lighten the load, to guide the way and to secure the future. Depend on him in faith!

Lord, grant me serenity knowing that you are with me always. Amen.

The Sovereign LORD is my strength; he makes my feet like the feet of a deer, he enables me to go on the heights. (Habakkuk 3:19)

A NEVER-FAILING SOURCE OF STRENGTH

Two men once visited a factory. The tour guide showed them the huge rooms where the machines were running and making a great deal of noise. Then the guide led them to a much smaller room where it was very quiet. One of the men said, "There isn't much going on in here, is there?" The guide smiled and replied, "This is the most important room of all. This is where the power comes from to run the great machines." With that the visitors looked in wonder at the huge, almost noiseless dynamos.

Our lives are often like a factory with its noise and activity. But perhaps we sometimes forget where the power source is and that if the power were not on we couldn't produce a thing. The Lord is our power source. The same power he used to create the world he uses today to keep all things in existence. "In him all things hold together," the Bible says (Colossians 1:17). God is not resting somewhere in the heavens, but he is constantly and actively present with us keeping and sustaining us, directing and governing us. "In him we live and move and have our being," Paul reminded the philosophers in Athens (Acts 17:28).

Habakkuk realized that. Habakkuk knew that if left on his own he would only tremble and falter. His heart would pound. His lips would quiver. Decay would creep into his bones, and his legs would tremble. But with the Lord as his strength he says he can run like a deer and bound up steep slopes. The Apostle Paul in his letter to the Philippians says the same thing in slightly different words. "I can do everything through him who gives me strength" (Philippians 4:13).

Dynamos can break down. Batteries can die. But the Lord is a never-failing source of strength.

The greatest thing of all is that by his strength the Lord redeemed us. It took more than a mere man to crush Satan's head and to defeat sin and death. It took the almighty Son of God, the God-man. By his own power Jesus rose victorious from the grave. By the gospel the Holy Spirit works powerfully in our hearts to bring us to faith in Jesus our Savior. By that same power he keeps our faith alive. By the Lord's strength we live our lives for him. By his strength and power the Lord will raise us from the dead and take us to eternal life in heaven. The Lord is our never-failing source of strength.

Lord God, keep us mindful that without you we can do nothing. Keep our faith alive and well, and give us strength to serve you faithfully. Amen.

"Is anything too hard for the Lord? I will return to you at the appointed time next year and Sarah will have a son." (Genesis 18:14)

WITH GOD NOTHING IS IMPOSSIBLE

Broken promises! How many times has not a promise been made to us that was never kept? Why so many broken promises? There are of course people who will just lie to us and never intend to make good on their promises. But there are also many sincere people who make promises but do not carry them out. One of the major reasons that there are so many broken promises is because the person, although he has good intentions, oftentimes finds that he is just unable to do what he has promised.

Let us be thankful that God and his promises are different. He never lacks the power or ability to carry them out. Solomon recognized this when he wrote in 1 Kings 8:56, "Praise be to the Lord. . . . Not one word has failed of all the good promises he gave."

We have already seen that God's promise to Abraham and Sarah was one such promise. God's great power and wisdom had no problem in rearranging the laws of nature, so that the child could be conceived and born. The miraculous birth of Isaac reminds us of the great miracle of the birth of Jesus, our Savior. Contrary to the laws of nature, Isaac was born.

He was born because God had promised it. Contrary to the laws of nature, Jesus was born. Again it was because God had made a promise: "Behold a virgin shall conceive and bear a son" (Isaiah 7:14).

God's power was at work to make sure what he had promised would come to pass. By God's power faith was worked in Sarah's heart. God also put his power to work in her body, to make sure that his precious promise would come to pass. In Hebrews 11:11 we read, "Through faith Sarah herself received renewed strength (power) to conceive seed, and was delivered of a child when she was past age." God's power fulfilled his precious promise.

"With God nothing shall be impossible." When we hear God's promises to us in our times of trouble, guilt and fear, we are to find the same comfort and assurance that Abraham and Sarah found. God will surely bring to pass by his power what he has promised.

The promise stands: "With God nothing shall be impossible," not the creation of the world, not the adorning of the heavens with millions of stars, and God be praised, not even the salvation of mankind!

Lord, move us always to trust each of your promises as sure and certain, because you have the almighty power to bring them to pass. Amen.

As a mother comforts her child, so will I comfort you; and you will be comforted over Jerusalem. (Isaiah 66:13)

COMFORT LIKE ONLY A MOTHER CAN

A toothless smile grins into the TV and mouths the words, "Hi, Mom!" The burly football player has just recovered a fumble in the big game. The isolation camera picks him out on the sideline and in the midst of his jubilation, the first person he thinks of is his mother—the woman who brought him into the world, the person to whom he owes so much.

Perhaps it is a natural instinct to recall those early childhood experiences, lost deep in the recesses of our subconscious. Then our two biggest worries, a full stomach and a dry diaper, were just taken care of automatically. Consequently the thought of mother remains a comforting fixture in our minds throughout our life.

So the Lord uses this expression to indicate his loving concern for the faithful remnant of Israel. Just as a mother consoles her child, God promises to take pity on his people. He will rescue them out of the Babylonian captivity which awaited the inhabitants of Judah not many years after Isaiah wrote. They will be restored to their native Jerusalem. It will be rebuilt and resettled seventy years after the destruction of the temple. Thus they will be comforted.

This is ancient history, of course. Because we know it happened just as the Lord said it would, we can be assured of his comforting love as well. We find ourselves in need of it quite frequently, in fact. When we have sinned and gone astray, each one to our own way, it is good to know that the Lord will come looking for us like a mother searches for a lost child. When we have fallen and hurt ourselves, because we stumbled carelessly over temptation, it is a warm feeling to be picked up and brushed off by the forgiving hands of the Lord. When we wake up frightened in the night of danger, it is reassuring to be able to call out to God for help and know that he is right there.

Earlier in Isaiah's book the Lord illustrates his love for us by comparing it to the bond that exists between a mother and child regardless of what intervenes over the years. "Can a mother forget the baby at her breast and have no compassion on the child she has borne? Though she may forget, I will not forget you" (Isaiah 49:15). Here we have a guarantee of comfort from our God to keep us ever content.

Loving God, we thank you for the comfort you have given to us in all circumstances of life. Amen.

The LORD said, ". . . I am concerned about their suffering." (Exodus 3:7)

GOD'S CONCERN FOR OUR SUFFERING

Have you ever been the object of concern? Showered with get-well cards and mobbed by visitors when ill? Overwhelmed with food, clothing and helping hands after a misfortune? Swamped with mail and telephone calls in grief? It's a heartwarming experience. It feels good to know others care and want to help. It brings hope during those dark hours.

Imagine what Moses must have felt when the living God from the burning bush said, "I am concerned about their suffering." The eternal Lord was aware of Israel's affliction. He cared and wanted to help them in their distress. The Lord's words raised hope in Moses. His people would receive help in their dark hours.

The Lord's words stirred up hope in the hearts of the suffering Israelites. Moses relayed the Lord's message to them. "And when they [the Israelites] heard that the Lord was concerned about them and had seen their misery, they bowed down and worshiped" (Exodus 4:31). The Lord's words offered them comfort and hope. The Israelites praised and worshiped the Lord.

Acquaintances are not always aware of our sufferings. Marriage faltering. Loneliness. Lack of self-confidence. Disobedient children. Bills overdue. More than likely we hear no expression of concern from others. We are not aware that others care and want to help. That makes suffering doubly painful.

There is One, however, who is concerned about our suffering. It is the One who cared for and wanted to help suffering Israel—the eternal Lord. Through his Word he says, "Never will I leave you; never will I forsake you," and "Call upon me in the day of trouble; I will deliver you." With these promises the eternal Lord is saying, "I am aware. I care. I want to help. I will help."

Do sufferings afflict us? Set aside for handy reference the eternal Lord's promises cited in the previous paragraph. Read them again when you need to know that someone is concerned. God's promises give comfort and raise hope during our dark hours.

Eternal Lord, during my sufferings may your promises remind me of your concern and your willingness to help. Amen.

So the Lord brought us out of Egypt with a mighty hand . . . and with miraculous signs and wonders. (Deuteronomy 26:8)

GOD DELIVERS HIS PEOPLE FROM HARM

The same mighty miracles with which God judged the Egyptians were also the means by which God delivered his people. When the first nine plagues fell on Egypt, God spared his people from harm. In the last plague, the angel of death passed over every home which had the blood of a lamb on the doorposts. God spared the firstborn sons in Israel from death.

At the Red Sea God parted the waters, so that his people could get safely to the other side and away from the pursuing Egyptian army. In joy the people sang, "The Lord is my strength and my song; he has become my salvation." In the desert when Israel had needs, God provided water and manna and quail. The people of Israel found joy in constantly calling to mind these mighty acts by which God delivered them from Egypt and rescued them from harm while on their way to the promised land.

Does God deliver us from harm in exactly the same way? Yes and no. Yes, sometimes we experience a miraculous deliverance from an accident or illness. But no, God does not always use miraculous means to deliver us from harm. He may use those whom he has placed over us, our parents or the government. No matter how he does it, he keeps his promise, "No harm will befall you."

This promise does not mean our lives will be free of trouble. It does mean that God will control and direct any trouble in our lives for our good. And in the midst of such trouble our Good Shepherd will give us the strength we need and will comfort us with his rod and his staff.

We know that God will deliver us completely from all harm when he takes us home to heaven. With Paul we can say, "The Lord will rescue me from every evil attack and will bring me safely to his heavenly kingdom." There we will sing Israel's song of deliverance one more time as we stand safely on the heavenly shore, "The Lord is my strength and my song; he has become my salvation."

Oh, magnify the Lord with me,
With me exalt His name!
When in distress to Him I cried,
He to my rescue came.
The hosts of God encamp around
The dwellings of the just;
Deliv'rance He affords to all
Who on His succor trust. Amen.

The LORD . . . be gracious to you. (Numbers 6:25)

GETTING WHAT WE DESERVE

Someone put it this way: Justice is getting what you deserve; mercy is not getting what you deserve; and grace is getting what you don't deserve.

That sums up the Christian faith pretty well. We are all sinners who continually have displeased and angered our Creator by breaking his commandments in our thoughts and words and deeds. Justice demands that we forever be banished from God's presence. But God is merciful and doesn't punish us with an eternity in hell. And then he takes it a step farther. Although none of us deserve God's love and blessing, that's exactly what he gives us—eternally. That's grace!

The Scriptures declare that the earth is filled with God's unfailing love or grace. We see this in the works of nature. The Lord God Almighty has created the heavens and the earth. In his grace he continues to care for his creation, even though it has fallen into sin. He sends the sunshine and rain to make the crops grow, so we have food to eat. He gives us our bodies, souls, minds and abilities. Our health, our wealth, our families, our friends—whatever we have is from our gracious God.

God's grace is most evident in our salvation. "We are justified freely by his grace," writes the Apostle Paul. Through the life, death and resurrection of Jesus Christ we enjoy God's grace.

As a young man John Newton was an unbeliever and a slave trader. By God's grace he came to faith in Christ. Newton was moved to write the beautiful hymn: "Amazing grace! how sweet the sound, that saved a wretch like me." Perhaps we have known God's grace so long that we take it for granted. We shouldn't. God's grace is equally amazing in each of our lives.

This whole notion runs counter to the spirit of our day which tells us just the opposite: "You deserve the best. . . . You're number one." Though the Bible starts by telling us how unworthy we are, it ends by giving us a dignity the world could never even conceive of. We can hold our heads up high. We know we are worthwhile. We own the best gifts God himself can offer. We are part of God's family and will live with him forever.

When you think about it, that's mind-boggling, isn't it? The Lord is gracious to us. We are getting what we don't deserve.

From all pain and imperfection,
Gracious Lord, deliver me,
Heaven's glory let me see.
Keep me under Thy direction
That the grace Thou gavest me
I may praise eternally. Amen.